WHAT YOUR COLLEAGUES ARE SAYING . . .

I have been a fan of Larry Thompson's work since I interviewed him on Corwin's Leaders Coaching Leaders *podcast.* Responsibility-Centered Discipline *is about discipline, but it's also about being more human, and we all need a little more of that.*

—**Peter DeWitt**, CEO Instructional Leadership Collective,
Corwin Author, Leadership Coach, Facilitator of Learning,
Education Week blogger, Albany, New York

This whole-school approach shows educators how to make the much-needed shift away from gaining control of students to helping students control themselves. To create a mindshift change throughout the school community, this book provides step-by-step actions to build skills such as responsibility, perseverance, empathy, and self-regulation in every learner from preK through high school. Every school leader should read this book and then buy it for every member of their staff.

—**Debbie Silver**, Author of *Fall Down 7 Times, Get Up 8*,
Co-author of *Deliberate Optimism: Still Reclaiming the Joy in Education*, Melissa, Texas

The need to reimagine school discipline has never been more important. Thompson lays out a clear pathway for school staff and students to engage in a manner that shifts the mindset and practice of school discipline to have a positive impact on the culture of any school. The Responsibility-Centered Discipline *approach is grounded in research and best practice. I encourage every educator to read it.*

—**Steven M. Constantino**, Executive Professor,
William & Mary School of Education, Author,
Engage Every Family: Five Simple Principles, Naples, Florida

In this post-pandemic era, teachers are coming to grips with the reality that classroom management strategies that worked pre-pandemic are not always as reliable as they used to be. This reality begs for contemporary strategies for the contemporary student. Responsibility-Centered Discipline *does just that and in doing so, goes far beyond short-term consequences. I endorse this book with zero hesitation nor reservation.*

—**Baruti Kafele**, Education Consultant, Author,
Retired Principal,
Orange City, New Jersey

Responsibility-Centered Discipline

Keeping Students on the Path of Accountability

Larry Thompson

For information:

Corwin
A Sage Company
2455 Teller Road
Thousand Oaks, California 91320
(800) 233-9936
www.corwin.com

Sage Publications Ltd.
1 Oliver's Yard
55 City Road
London EC1Y 1SP
United Kingdom

Sage Publications India Pvt. Ltd.
Unit No 323-333, Third Floor, F-Block
International Trade Tower Nehru Place
New Delhi 110 019
India

Sage Publications Asia-Pacific Pte. Ltd.
18 Cross Street #10-10/11/12
China Square Central
Singapore 048423

Vice President and Editorial Director: Monica Eckman
Senior Acquisitions Editor: Tanya Ghans
Content Development Manager: Desirée A. Bartlett
Senior Editorial Assistant: Nyle De Leon
Production Editor: Vijayakumar
Copy Editor: Tammy Giesmann
Typesetter: TNQ Tech Pvt. Ltd.
Proofreader: Girish Sharma
Indexer: TNQ Tech Pvt. Ltd.
Cover Designer: Janet Kiesel
Marketing Manager: Melissa Duclos

Printed in the United States of America

Paperback ISBN 978-1-0719-2495-2

This book is printed on acid-free paper.

24 25 26 27 28 10 9 8 7 6 5 4 3 2 1

Contents

About the Author

Larry Thompson is a popular speaker, author, and thought leader in the field of education and leadership training. Often called upon to deliver keynote presentations for state and national conferences, leaders immediately connect with Larry's knowledge, humor, and passion. As the creator of Responsibility-Centered Discipline (RCD), Responsibility-Centered Leadership (RCL), and Responsibility-Centered Parenting (RCP), he has worked with thousands of educators, leaders, and parents throughout the country and outside of the United States. He was a former state principal of the year. He is nationally recognized as a leading educator who has created an innovative system for success in parenting, business, and education.

Introduction

IF NOT NOW, WHEN?

Ask any educator worth their salt and they will say that classroom management is a vital skill for teachers to have if they want to run a successful classroom. They will say that it doesn't matter how well a teacher understands the content or pedagogy if they cannot create a culture of joyful order. Yet teacher training programs tend to spend most of their focus on instruction and content with very little attention given to classroom management. When it is discussed, lesson engagement and relationship building are said to be the key to preventing virtually all behavior problems. The underlying message new teachers receive is students will not misbehave if you prepare highly engaging lessons and deliver quality instruction. While there is no denying the impact of engaging instruction on the creation of a productive learning environment, even the most skilled teachers are likely to encounter student behaviors that are disruptive, disengaged, or unproductive. Students will continue to bring the challenges of life to the classroom. Their lives have trauma, emotional challenges, and even mental health issues. The overreliance on the engaging lessons narrative to prevent disruptive behavior leaves many teachers discouraged when classroom management issues inevitably arise. Teachers begin to question if they are good enough for this job. The last few years have seen the fallout of this message (along with many other issues) contributing to high levels of principal and teacher burnout.

The Responsibility-Centered Discipline (RCD) framework was born out of the necessity to respond to the pressing challenges that schools are facing daily in classrooms, hallways, cafeterias, playgrounds, time-out rooms, and more. For well over ten years and across dozens of schools and districts, this framework has transformed students' behavior in schools. While it helps all students grow their confidence, RCD really kicks into gear when the first level of preventative strategies does not work for a student. At its heart, RCD is all about building a student's agency and giving them the tools to better understand who they are, and which tools are best for them.

Does society need to make changes overall for school systems? Without a doubt. The question is, how do schools support students in need right now? Learning how to productively solve problems, even if the problem is not a person's fault, will always be an important life skill. When schools adopt this mentality, it is not long before students internalize a sustained growth mindset for improved behavior. The following story is told by Kevin. Kevin is currently a school leader. His first year of high school coincided with my first year as a principal at this building.

MEET KEVIN

I grew up in a small rural farming community in Kansas where my family makeup and structure were atypical. My mom was White, and my dad was African American. At the time my father moved to the community, he was one of only four African Americans. My parents divorced when I was five, yet another contributing factor that made me feel different from my classmates.

My older brother, whom I idolized, was four years older than me and finishing up his senior year. Throughout high school, my brother didn't always make the best choices. He had run-ins with law enforcement, and his fair share of detentions and suspensions. I don't think my brother's teachers meant any harm, but the strategies they used to get him to meet their expectations usually generated more anger. The harder they tightened the screws, the harder he fought back. This damaged many relationships with his teachers. He hated school, and he didn't have any motivation to achieve at a high level academically.

As I was finishing eighth grade, and preparing for high school, I assumed my experience would be like my brother's. In fact, I was excited to make the teachers' lives difficult. My goal was to wreak as much havoc and chaos as possible. In my mind, I felt that none of the teachers at the high school cared about me, my brother, or my family. So soon after starting high school, I wanted to send a clear message to the staff with some friends. The plan was to ask to leave the classroom during first period and zip tie all the freshman lockers shut. After completing the mission, I went back to my classroom. After the bell rang, I rushed to the lockers and was ecstatic to see absolute chaos unfolding as students struggled to figure out how to get the things they needed out of their lockers. Feeling like a criminal mastermind, I made my way to my next class.

It wasn't more than five minutes into class when the phone rang. The teacher shook his head and told me I needed to go to the office. I was excited because this was going to be my first opportunity to send a message to the principal that what they had done with my brother was not going to work on me either. Unbeknownst to me, the leadership at the high school had changed. Larry Thompson had become our new principal. He had begun laying the groundwork for a new way to work through classroom discipline challenges. He was in the early stages of implementing Responsibility-Centered Discipline (RCD) at our high school.

As I sat down, Larry listened to me. He worked with me in a way that held me accountable, yet he was still caring and supportive. This conversation came across as authentic and genuine. He guided the conversation in a way that led me to realize my poor choices and helped me figure out how I could begin to solve the problem I had created. I didn't know I needed a mentor in life until after that conversation. I had constructed such high and thick walls around myself based on my perceptions of the adults in my high school. Mr. Thompson was able to break those walls down and it was the start of what would become one of the most supportive relationships in my life. For the first time in my life, it felt like an adult outside of my house cared for me.

As educators, you never know how much impact you have in a student's story. Larry (I no longer call him Mr. Thompson) had a tremendous impact on my journey. The culture and community that he established through the implementation of RCD transformed the building in so many ways. I witnessed, as a student, how our teachers began to work with us when we made mistakes. Because it was so different from what we were accustomed to, many of us referred to this as "the quiet talk." In years before, we were used to being called out publicly. Now our teachers would speak to us privately. Even though we joked about getting the "quiet talk," we preferred it to the former methods. The teachers in our school began to build deeper relationships with us as students and made us feel valued and supported.

After this experience, I too wanted to be somebody who played that type of positive role in students' lives. I knew I wanted to be an educator. I later became a high school teacher, and early on discovered I, too, had a knack for working with challenging students. I went on to become a school administrator, and I now use the RCD program that worked so well for me.

Responsibility-Centered Discipline not only builds consistency in expectations for students, but it also builds consistency in teachers' ability to address students when the expectations are not met. Because RCD is a systemic change, the behaviors are consistently coached at all behavior intensity levels, from a side chat in the class to a student whose behavior warrants removal from the room. The RCD framework helps educators increase their confidence when a student shows resistance so fewer students are placed out of class. The result is more students enjoying a space where respectfulness is a guiding principle that is expected and required by everyone in their school. Many students and staff in RCD schools communicate that after RCD is implemented, the entire building feels calmer. More people seem happy and relationships with students seem stronger.

HOW THIS BOOK IS ORGANIZED

Chock full of practical steps and illustrations, this book takes school leaders through a step-by-step process to understand and begin implementing Responsibility-Centered Discipline (RCD) in their school. It is important to note that RCD pairs well with the average school day and most behavioral programs or systems. There is no question that this process requires a mind shift, but once the shift is made it is adaptable to a school's current practices.

Chapters 1 and 2 give an overview of the RCD process and define key terms. They delve into what psychology has long known about how well-regulated brains are supported and how this knowledge can be leveraged for students.

Chapters 3 to 7 outline the four main components of RCD: the foundations, the six exits students use to avoid responsibility, a structured conversation to return students to a path of responsibility, and the creation of a solutions space. The fourth step of the process is broken into two chapters (Chapters 6 and 7) to adequately describe its implementation.

Chapter 8 concludes with a high-level view for how school leaders can prepare to lead this change in their building.

PART I

Defining RCD's Key Concepts

CHAPTER ONE

Responsibility-Centered Discipline

Defining RCD

COMING UP IN THIS CHAPTER . . .

- **What RCD is and what RCD is not**
- **What makes RCD unique**
- **Key concepts**
- **Autonomy, mastery, purpose**
- **Algorithmic versus heuristics**

Most schools today exist in a sort of Bermuda Triangle of school discipline. When people think of the Bermuda Triangle, many things come to mind: ships disappear, planes go down never to be seen again, navigational equipment quits working and things disappear off the radar only to reappear again elsewhere. How do schools resemble the Bermuda Triangle? The three points of the actual Bermuda Triangle are replaced by the student, the teacher, and the administration. The chaos begins when a difficult situation arises between a student and a teacher in the classroom, and if the situation is problematic enough, the principal gets involved. Because the principal(s) did not see the event, they do not really know how it went down. This can cause the administration to question how it may have been handled. Leaders may say things that illustrate this doubt such as, *"Why didn't this teacher just talk to the kid?"* or *"I bet I know which classroom this student came from."* Because the teacher cannot hear what is taking place in the office, this can cause them to begin to doubt the leader. This is demonstrated in frequently heard statements from classroom teachers such as, *"I don't even know where that kid is, I sent them out two days ago."* Or *"I don't know what they did with this kid, but they walked back in with a candy in their mouth!"*

All parties are doing the best they can, but a lack of coherence in how behavior is managed causes dysfunction. Specifically, school leaders and their staff begin to mistrust one another.

Adding to the issue of poor consistency and transparency are two competing theories that dominate educator beliefs about the best ways to get students to improve their behaviors. *The Heart* or *The Hammer* is one way to conceptualize these theories. The hammer theory believes that being tougher on the student can drive a change in behavior. The heart theory believes that if good relationships are established, students will inevitably improve their behavior. These two groups of educators are often at odds with one another and, at times, at odds with the administration:

The Hammer

The problem is we just coddle kids today.
No one is accountable for their actions in this school.

The Heart

Some teachers don't want to get to know the kids the way they need to.
Don't these teachers understand trauma?

Principals can find themselves trying to appease these two groups to keep staff on board. Said one principal, "I think my job has become either rescuing students from the angry teacher or rescuing the teacher from the angry kid."

The hard part is helping the "warring factions" see that neither the heart nor the hammer perspective reliably predicts outcomes. This is easy to test: Ask a group of teachers to raise their hand if they have ever seen a consequence work, and almost every hand in the room will go up. Then ask the same group if they have ever seen a consequence not work, and every hand will go up. Ask if they have seen a relationship with a student change the behavior, and most hands will go up. Then ask if they have witnessed a student become more manipulative when a relationship is formed, or if they know of a student who will not let anyone get passed their guard long enough to build a relationship? Again, almost every hand goes up. This proves that these approaches to student behavior are hit-or-miss.

Proponents of Responsibility-Centered Discipline believe it is time to reassess our classrooms and give leaders and teachers the skills to feel prepared for these challenging moments. With a new set of skills, educators can make good outcomes more predictable, instead of a roll of the dice. Rather than relying too heavily on *The Heart* or *The Hammer* which are hit-or-miss, true change comes from engaging a process in the student's brain. The following is an introduction to concepts that are essential for Responsibility-Centered Discipline. Subsequent chapters will discuss each in more depth.

A NEW APPROACH: DEFINING RESPONSIBILITY-CENTERED DISCIPLINE (RCD)

In 2011, Daniel Pink wrote *Drive: The Surprising Truth About What Motivates Us*. The guiding principles for RCD are heavily influenced by the framework in *Drive* focused on enabling people to become intrinsically motivated, through the internal drivers of autonomy, mastery, and purpose (more on this later). Most importantly, it posits that the goals that people set for themselves and that are devoted to attaining mastery are usually healthy and well-sustained over time.

Responsibility-Centered Discipline is all about helping students ignite their intrinsic motivation to be a valuable member of the school community, with educator support. First, RCD views productive behavior as a skill that can be learned as opposed to something students are born with, much like Carol Dweck's growth mindset work (2007). Just like a student can improve in reading, math, or science with the right instruction, so can their behavior improve with the proper guidance. While most educators know this intellectually, in the heat of a challenging moment, this knowledge is easily obscured. This is because in these tense moments, it can be very difficult for an educator to determine: (1) what a student is trying to communicate (which can often be different from what they are saying), (2) the right response that won't escalate or minimize the problem, and (3) when an issue is too big to handle at the classroom level. The RCD process, illustrated in Figure 1.1, provides guidance for all this.

RESPONSIBILITY-CENTERED DISCIPLINE PROCESS

1. Lay the **school's foundations** which are a few simple goals that the entire staff wants to strengthen in every student.
2. Understand the **six exits** that both students and teachers commonly use that get in the way of students taking responsibility for their behavior.
3. Use a guided conversation, consisting of **five points (Give 'em Five),** to help students take responsibility for changing their behavior.
4. Have a **solutions space** ready for students who need additional help. This is a reimagining of the in-school suspension rooms prevalent in schools.

FIGURE 1.1 • Responsibility-Centered Discipline Implementation Process

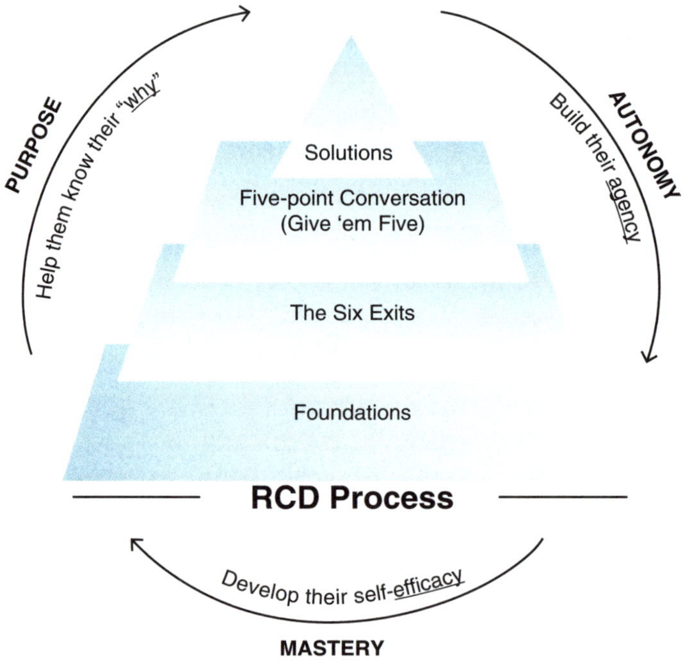

Source: AccuTrain

RCD is a systemic approach to school discipline wherein all adults in the building have a common language, clear protocols, and a working knowledge of which behaviors require which responses. Principals, teachers, students, and other key support staff have a clear role to play in the process. When the situation calls for a student to leave the classroom, RCD creates trust across the building for how the situation will be handled. Staff can have faith that whoever worked with a student did their best to figure out the problem's root causes and offer the student the opportunity to come up with a viable solution.

It should be said now, and often, that RCD is not about getting rid of consequences or keeping students in the classroom or school at any cost. It is about finding lasting solutions to problems that students create and own. The goal of RCD is to take advantage of challenging moments with students and turn them into learning opportunities. While the approach is good for all students, it is especially designed for students who do not respond to the standard culture-building processes put in place at many schools.

As the name implies, responsibility is the main focus of RCD. Quite literally, the ideas in this process are all about helping students gain the *ability* to *respond* in a manner that can create lasting change. Educators already know that it is important not to take learning processes for granted when teaching students. They understand that good teaching is often about making the invisible, visible. RCD gives educators a common language and a system for making the habits of de-escalation, self-regulation, and good decision-making transparent for students.

WHAT RCD IS NOT

Creating a Responsibility-Centered Culture should be thought of as journey, not a race. It is very different from "making kids behave." RCD is not a fix-kids-quick scheme, but a transformative shift in how schools think about school discipline. There are no points, no treats for good behavior (although children are celebrated for mastering skills), no "sticks" to force kids to behave (although there are consequences as needed; "sticks" and consequences are not synonymous), no elaborate conversations with peers are required (although these are welcomed as a school sees fit). In general, while RCD does believe that some of these common practices are counterproductive, it does not ask schools to outright abandon these practices—few things are off the table. It does ask schools to reflect on how effective these practices have been, especially with their more challenging students.

RCD is also not scripted. Learning a few quick, catchy phrases is not a skill. When a script is used, it is easy to unintentionally communicate to students that they are not being listened to.

Students need to feel heard to get their brain in a position for problem-solving. RCD has enough structure that every teacher knows the framework for coaching through a challenging behavior but is given enough freedom, so their voice and personality are still in the conversation. This means that two people using the skill can sound very different. Lastly, RCD is not about how to help educators remove themselves from the conflict, but how to step into it with skill and support for the student who may not have enough skill to do this on their own.

HOW RCD IS UNIQUE

Figure 1.2 lists some key differences between RCD and other popular approaches. Once again, few strategies are off limits. This includes offering rewards, giving consequences, using restorative practices, or even issuing expulsions. There can be a time and place for some of these, and RCD is often complementary to these practices.

FIGURE 1.2 • RCD's Unique Approach

POPULAR MANAGEMENT STRATEGIES	RCD APPROACH
Clip Charts (red, yellow, green)	• Private, individualized plans • Student self-assessment
Restorative Circle Talks	• Restoration fostered through student-generated solutions as opposed to apologies • Designed to fit into typical school schedule • Activates heuristic process
Zero tolerance	• Pairs solutions with consequences • Differentiates based on circumstances and student needs
Point Stores/Incentives	• Emphasis on internal motivation to build lasting change • Self-assessing • Celebrating student growth

The second half of this chapter will go a little deeper into autonomy, mastery, and purpose because these concepts are the heartbeat of this work. Most educators want their students to become self-motivated and find the internal strength to do hard things in school and life. However, many educators, even parents, have been trained or believe that when self-motivation is absent, rewards and consequences will do the job. However, these often do little if the brain is not put in a position for growth. What really gets students on the path to be their best self is feeling proud of hard work (mastery) and understanding their personal why (purpose).

FOCUS ON AUTONOMY

Autonomy is the desire for humans to be in control of themselves. Surprise! The opposite of autonomy is dependence or even subjugation, and human nature tends to push against these emotions. When a student begins to feel controlled, they will often begin to fight for autonomy. For example, a teacher might tell a student they will not get recess this afternoon and the student responds with, "That's okay. It's too hot outside, and I wanted to stay in any way." Or if a student is told they won't get to go on a zoo trip if they don't behave and the student replies, "I went to the zoo this summer and it was boring. They don't even have monkeys anymore." Educators need to notice this stance and not simply categorize the behavior as disrespectful. In the last example, the student really does want to go to the zoo, but the part of the brain activated by the teacher's threats is the fight for autonomy. Once someone begins to fight for autonomy, the brain only cares about one thing, and that is not relinquishing control. Students can become very irrational in these moments.

FOCUS ON MASTERY

Mastery is the part within humans that wants to show the ability to tackle a challenge that takes effort, focus, and persistence. This part is often easy to recognize in young students. It sounds like this:

- "Did you read my paper yet?"
- "You should hang this one up!"
- "Did you hear about my game?"

They want to share that they can do hard things that take skill. Educators often activate the part of the child's brain that feels strong when they *don't* do a request instead of feeling strong when they *do* what is asked of them. The following is an example of how two teachers set the class up for an autonomy fight versus a mastery accomplishment:

NON-EXAMPLE

The Autonomy Fight

Teacher A

> Class we are getting ready to line up. It is important not to touch other people. No one wants to be touched and I need your hands and feet kept to yourself. So, when we go to art, keep your hands and feet to yourself. If you don't do that then you'll need to practice hands and feet to yourself at recess time.

Here's what happens: At least a few kids sneakily start touching someone in front or behind them, just to show they can. This teacher unintentionally activated some of the students' need for autonomy; feeling strong meant not meeting the goal. The student's need for autonomy results in them not doing what is asked to show the teacher they cannot be controlled.

EXAMPLE

A Mastery Accomplishment

Teacher B

> Class we are going to go to art soon. We want to be respectful, and I know sometimes it can be hard to remember to keep our hands and feet in our own space when we are in the hallways. Before we get up, let's do a quick assessment on ourselves. Think to yourself, am I a "one," which means it is a little too hard for me. Or are you at a "two"? This means I may need a reminder or coaching. A "three" means I can do it all by myself. Last is a "four." This is easy for me, and I can help others. Now think of where you are right now on this. Once you decide, would the threes and fours please line up first and I will walk with those who feel they may need some coaching.

Most likely result: all students lined up and in the mastery part of the brain, desiring to demonstrate they are strong by meeting the goal.

FOCUS ON PURPOSE

Educators are often asked to find their "why." Students need to know their why too. When students feel needed, impactful, and understand the personal benefits of their behaviors, they are more internally driven. Everyone has witnessed a student who rises to the occasion when given the job of helping someone else such as reading to younger students or helping a teacher with a project. Purpose is the reason most educators chose the profession. They want to make a difference and leave a legacy they can be proud of. Often, teachers give all the "purposeful" responsibilities to students who already have it together. Teachers can forget that all students want to feel purposeful, and that the seeds of purpose can live inside even the most challenging moments.

DOES THE STUDENT NEED AN ALGORITHM OR A HEURISTIC?

The last two key concepts to keep in mind before diving into the RCD are algorithms and heuristics. When a person is asked to complete a task, the solution will either be algorithmic or heuristic. An algorithmic task means the "task has an established instruction down a single pathway to one conclusion" (Pink, 2011). Think of a mathematical formula. Know the formula, solve the problem.

If there is no algorithm, then a heuristic process is needed. This usually means a person must experiment with possibilities and devise their own novel solution. One example is time management. For some, time management is easy. If the meeting is at 9:00 a.m., they begin to think of how long the drive is, what time they should leave the house, and ultimately arrive on time. The process is done without much effort. However, a large percentage of people struggle with being on time. A person who struggles to be on time will likely not get better through consequences. A heuristic process must be activated. Setting the clock ahead by 10 minutes is one way, or they can tell themselves the meeting is at 8:30 a.m. instead of 9:00 a.m. These strategies make little sense to punctual people but can work perfectly for the chronically late.

PRO TIP

It is common for educators to coach behavior from their own algorithms and tell a student how to change based on how the educator would solve the problem. It is important to position the student's brain to create its own heuristic.

When schools respond ineffectively to student behavior, it is difficult to get a student's brain to move to a heuristic process. RCD leaves the door open for the student's brain to find its own unique heuristic to master the skill.

Key Takeaways

- The current ways we approach behavior are hit-or-miss at effectiveness.
- RCD is not a quick fix but a transformative shift. The goal is to take advantage of challenging behavioral moments and turn them into lifelong learning opportunities.
- This is a skills-based framework where educators learn to step into the conflict cycle to support students who do not have enough skills to do so on their own.
- To internally motivate students, we must ensure our educators understand the significance of autonomy, mastery, and purpose. All students desire autonomy, need mastery moments, and need to feel they have purpose.
- If a student does not have the algorithm, then make the task a heuristic process which means the student will need to experiment with possibilities and devise their own novel solution.

MEET JEREMY

Jeremy was a kindergarten student who struggled with respecting others' space. His teacher tried using rewards and consequences to get him to keep his hands and feet to himself, especially when walking in the hallways with his classmates.

Jeremy's teacher was desperate to figure out how to help him. She had taken away his recess so many times that he had learned how to counter this punishment with indifference: "I didn't want to go outside anyway. It's cold (or hot, or wet)." Or "I wanted to stay inside anyway."

Seeing that punishments were ineffective, she decided to take a more positive approach. As an alternative to taking away his recess, she would reward Jeremy if he changed his behavior. This worked for a few days, but as soon as he was not able to meet the expectations, he once again countered with indifference: "I don't even like that kind of candy." Now, just withholding a reward felt like a punishment to Jeremy.

After learning the RCD framework, the teacher began with "Jeremy, I know you can be a good friend to your classmates. Touching others while we are walking in the halls is causing some kids to not want to be your partner or walk near you in the halls. When I see that I can trust you to respect others' space, then I'll know I can also trust you to walk down the hall on your own. For now, I'll have you walk with me. Think of a plan so I can trust you in the halls. Let me know when you have your plan, so you can share it with me, and we can see if you are ready to walk by yourself again. I'll be anxious to hear your plan."

For the next few days, she walked alongside Jeremy, not with the motivation to embarrass him, but to be supportive. She reminded him of the personal benefit he would get of being with his friends, when he solved this problem.

One day, as the class was getting ready to head down the hallway, Jeremy walked over to his teacher and said, "I want to walk with my friends. I have a plan. I brought buttons from home."

The teacher was confused. "Buttons?"

Jeremy explained, "When I walk down the hall, I'll play with the buttons in my pockets and that will keep my hands busy. They will remind me to keep my hands to myself."

"That sounds like a great plan, Jeremy. But what will you do if you lose your buttons?"

He smiled proudly, "I already thought of that. If I lose them, I will just hold on to the inside of my pockets instead."

"That sounds like a great plan, Jeremy!"

Now, just imagine what Jeremy must have looked like as he walked down the hallway with his buttons—so proud of himself for his plan, and for being able to accomplish this successfully.

The **autonomy** of coming up with his own solution, the **mastery** of getting better at being successful in meeting his goal and the **purpose** in this case, the personal benefit of becoming better at making friends and being able to walk on his own. This made all the difference in Jeremy's behavior. Not only did his behavior improve, but greater trust and a more positive educator-student relationship was forged.

CONSIDER THIS...

Every Team Needs a Captain

A successful team has known components that make it rise above other teams. First, it has a strong team captain. For schools, that's the principal. This captain knows when to encourage, model, correct, and guide the teammates to help improve the team. A strong captain knows the players and even understands what each needs to improve. They have clear roles for each teammate and clear expectations for each member. Each team member knows their part while also trusting the others to know their parts. When a team is functioning at its best it can surpass expectations. RCD will give teams (staff) the clear path to lead each member to growth with clear expectations, practice feedback, and support. They will learn to trust the leader's role in behavior management and can accomplish far beyond what most educators have seen in schools. When this occurs the results are motivating, and staff often rediscover their purpose.

Ready, captains?

CHAPTER TWO

Self-Control

Elevating an Essential Skill

COMING UP IN THIS CHAPTER . . .

- How RCD builds self-control
- Over-spotting versus under-spotting
- Consequences versus accountability

For a long time, schools were all about academic skills and having the basic knowledge to do tasks that might show up on the job one day. Then corporations began seeing a gap and called on schools to teach the soft skills needed to thrive in the workplace (Mullane, 2022). These skills include punctuality, completing tasks, respect toward colleagues, productive collaboration in addition to many others. One study found that self-control to be the soft skill most backed up by science to have an impact on workplace success (Lippman et al., 2015). To be clear, this book is not about preparing students for the workplace. It is about training teachers to strengthen a student's self-control for school and for life. Educators cannot simply call for self-control and expect it to appear; it is not like teaching a content lesson. The old mindset of "If we teach it, they should be able to do it" doesn't produce results.

Everyone knows children have different levels of self-control. Students who are "good" turn in work on time, give their best effort, get along with others, show integrity, and are respectful. But some students are just the opposite. Often educators think that they can give these students more of what they give the stronger students to help them regain control, so they deploy the same strategy repeatedly. When the student does not change, the situation escalates and, for some students, expulsion becomes a possibility. While expulsion is sometimes needed to keep staff safe, the need for this action can be avoided with proper intervention. We would like to see an intervention that involves a shift away from gaining control of students to students gaining control of themselves. This is what will empower students to be successful now and in the future.

ELEVATING SELF-CONTROL

Almost every school mission statement states something about preparing students for their future. It is important to consider what that really means. There are two strong predictors of a student's future success: IQ and self-discipline (self-control) (Duckworth & Seligman, 2005). It is hard for educators to have an impact on a student's IQ, but there is much that can be done regarding self-control. This is very important, because while it is difficult to change IQ, the ability to acquire knowledge is more malleable. Students who acquire lots of knowledge are likely to fare better in life, and self-control is an important factor in knowledge acquisition.

School leaders must determine how many of the students performing low academically truly can't do the work and how many don't have the skills to get themselves to do the work. Not only is there a substantial difference, but there is a thread between the two that is often missed. If a student is genuinely struggling with certain concepts, and the teacher is prepared to scaffold the work, the students will still need to choose to focus on the work. Scaffolding may make this focus easier, but it alone does not guarantee a student will engage with a task. At some point every student will encounter work they find boring, too hard, or just don't feel like doing. That feeling is thoroughly human. It is what students do with these emotions when confronted with them that often separates success from failure. Technology is an example of misunderstanding engagement. Schools have learned the hard way that putting an iPad in a student's hands who has low self-control will often only make things more challenging.

What if school leaders and teachers have been tackling this problem the wrong way? Educators have exhausted themselves trying new techniques to get learning to happen.

In other words, there's a lot of adult effort and not enough focus on raising student effort. When the student is stronger in using self-control, the academic practices have a better chance of bringing success.

Furthermore, because educators have little training on how to strengthen self-control, students who demonstrate low self-control are often labeled as unmotivated, lazy, or disrespectful. They are frequently removed from class in the hopes it will be a wakeup call for the student. What really happens is the same students end up in the hallway or the office day after day.

BUILDING SELF-CONTROL BY SPOTTING

While there have been some recent stirrings that self-control does not work exactly like a muscle, the consensus from many scholars in the field is that this remains the best analogy. Roy F. Baumeister, a social psychologist known for his work on willpower, self-control, and self-esteem, and how they relate to human morality & success, sums it up well in a 2015 article from *Scientific American*:

> Over that time, I have come to the conclusion that self-control, which might also be referred to as self-regulation or willpower, works something like a muscle does. In particular, it seems to "tire" after a workout ... [But]willpower has not entirely vanished. Rather the body seems to be conserving energy; if an important challenge or opportunity arises, more self-control can be tapped ... Self-control can also strengthen with practice, as shown when people go through an exercise program to enhance it.

Regarding the benefits, see more from the same article:

> The ability to regulate our impulses and desires is indispensable to success in living and working with others. People with good control over their thought processes, emotions, and behaviors not only flourish in school and in their jobs but are also healthier, wealthier, and more popular. What is more, they are less likely to go astray by getting arrested, becoming addicted to drugs, or experiencing unplanned pregnancies.

Because self-control is like a muscle, it is important to know how to strengthen it for students. Think about a person lifting weights; they will get stronger if they stick with it.

Or will they? When an individual is lifting heavy weights, they should have a person spotting them. The spotter's job is to be there to keep them safe and provide the right amount of support. The spotter lifts the minimal amount for that goal to be achieved. If the spotter lifts too much, the goal won't be met. The muscles did not have to do enough work. In this book, this is referred to as over-spotting. Another possibility is the spotter may not help enough. The weight may end up stuck, and the lifter, once again, does not gain any strength. This is under-spotting.

OVER-SPOTTING

An over-spotting teacher tends to have a big heart and a strong desire to help the student, but they offer too much help. So, the paper gets finished with hours of support, the project is completed after many delays and reminders, and to the teacher, it feels like the goal is met. But the goal of the student gaining strength has not been met. It's a façade.

Examples of over-spotting:

- The student struggles with writing and refuses to do the work. The teacher has the student say what they want in the paper, and the teacher writes all their ideas down.
- A student has a problem with sharing the football at recess. The teacher brings another football from home for them to play with.
- A student refuses to work with the partner the teacher assigns. The teacher allows the student to pick their partner for partner activities from then on.

UNDER-SPOTTING

The under-spotting teacher often gets frustrated and will not lift enough of the weight for the student to meet the goals. This can sound like, "I am done with this kid. I guess they can just take this class again this summer." When frustrated enough, a teacher can even seem like they are pushing down when a child tries to lift the weight.

Examples of under-spotting:

- A student struggles with writing and shuts down in frustration. The teacher does not allow them to do recess or other activities until it is done.

- A student gets mad at other kids, and yells at them. The teacher puts the student in a desk away from the other kids for being disrespectful.
- The teacher sends the student to the hallway for the remainder of the period for talking too much.

Principals must lead the shift in their buildings to help staff become the perfect spotters of behavior. It starts by providing them with the skills to spot students' behaviors in a way that all students show gains in this area by the end of a school year.

BUILDING THE MUSCLE OF SELF-CONTROL

Think of self-control as a muscle that must get lots of strategic practice to grow. This involves repetitions with the correct amount of spotting. But many students have experienced models of discipline that allowed them to avoid lifting their problems. Therefore, a systemic approach is a must. If not, students will seek out over-spotters, or they will push for consequences to do the work for them. Anything that solves the problem other than the child, is not really solving the problem.

When the entire school's system is trained in building the students' muscles of self-control, it resembles a school that teaches academics in a highly systematic and skilled manner. If all students begin learning a foreign language in kindergarten, they have a great chance for being fluent by high school graduation. Picture what a school looks like that knows the process of providing repetitions for students to strengthen them week by week. Schools using the RCD method have seen this. It looks like one hundred percent of students proficient in reading in a high school, graduation rates increased by fifty-three percent, and a zero percent staff turnover rate.

PUTTING IN THE TIME

Great stuff rarely happens overnight. Because self-control is like a muscle, it will also fatigue, and students will complain about the new lifting they have to do. They may even ask for consequences in an effort to avoid the lifting. Don't be surprised if a student says, "Can't you just give me a consequence?" To this statement, respond, "If you still feel you need a consequence after you've solved this, we can talk about it then." Students rarely want the consequence, what they want is way out of the hard work of growing.

At the onset of implementing this framework, it is vital to acknowledge the incremental gains students make throughout the school year. The mastery part of the child's brain will be activated when they see their strength growing. They will start making comments such as, "I finished my paper on time," "I walked away from the fight," or "Did you see me helping a teacher this morning?"

When we build muscle, it has memory. Meaning, even after a break it responds faster than someone whose muscles have never been strengthened. This muscle will last in students and can be life changing for their future success. Most students with strong self-control have a good chance of living fulfilling lives. They can delay gratification, work hard even when they don't feel like it, and get along with all kinds of people. Schools who work to strengthen the muscle of self-control in students, will see them grow in skills and confidence.

CONSEQUENCES VERSUS ACCOUNTABILITY

For educators to strengthen their student's self-control, they must tease apart the difference between consequences and accountability. What most educators desire is personal accountability from students. What they often get is student accountability for serving a consequence, not for changing their behavior. Remember, RCD sees behavior as a skill and the goal is to help students understand it as a skill too. The myth that consequences equal accountability must be dispelled.

INCORPORATING ACCOUNTABILITY INTO CONSEQUENCES

PRO TIP

Ask, "Did the consequence we gave the student require them to do any work, any heavy lifting?" If not, the muscle will not gain strength.

For example, a student is not ready to be back into a space they've disrupted until they have a plan for their behavior to change. A plan is not, "I won't do it again," but rather an articulation of how they will stop themself from repeating the behavior when tempted (more on how to do this in later chapters). Sending a student back into a similar situation without a plan is almost a guarantee the problem will reoccur, subjecting students to more severe punishments for repeated offenses.

So, what should educators do with the student while they are trying to figure out a plan or when a student will not work on a plan? This is a common question, especially when RCD is new. Students are accustomed to fighting for autonomy and they don't see the mastery in solving hard problems yet. This is where pausing comes in. Students are given a pause until they have enough strength to be back in the setting that was problematic for them. For example, if recess is a temptation and often the student is too rough with other students, then the pause may be playing in a supervised area until they have an idea of how to play more safely with others. It is now up to them when they can return to the larger setting.

THE POWER OF PAUSING

Pausing the situation is more powerful than doling out a punishment. If the situation is paused (long enough for the student to do the required heavy lifting), the experience can become a mastery moment. Many of the most challenging students are used to the "cat and mouse game" of behavior, which is the autonomy fight. The teacher does an action and student figures out how to outmaneuver. With this new approach, it will take a while for students to realize they are not being tricked but instead being set up to solve their own problems. Pausing provides the time and space for building self-control. When they've come up with a plan they will have a tool to thwart impulsive, counterproductive habits.

PRO TIP

Some of our most challenging students may need intensive spotting as the muscle of self-control is weak. Students with trauma and emotional challenges will need spotting in ways that align to their specific needs. Educators need to be trained in how to understand and recognize children in trauma. (See *Help for Billy* (2012) by Heather Forbes for more information on supporting students with trauma.)

Key Takeaways

- To empower students to be successful, shift from a mindset of trying to gain control of students to students gaining control of themselves.
- Self-control is like a muscle. To grow the muscle of self-control, repeatedly practice using the muscle supported by the correct amount of spotting.
- Guide our educators to become the perfect spotters. The most caring teachers can over-spot students while those who lean toward consequences tend to under-spot students.
- Consequences do not necessarily mean accountability. Often the student is held accountable for the consequence but not the behavior. Make sure consequences allow the student to do majority of the heavy lifting.

MEET CARLOS

Carlos was a senior in high school and was sent to the alternative school upon returning from an expulsion at his local high school. He brought his anger and frustrations with him to the new school. This school was an RCD school and when his behaviors caused him to leave class he would go through the solutions process. Often, he would have multiple office referrals during one week. Slowly he began to find his own (heuristic) ways to manage his anger and he even became a leader for younger students in the school. The principal was focused on the students getting stronger in their level of self-control and knew Carlos was ready for the next step with his new skills. The principal met with Carlos and told him he was ready to try a class back at his high school. Carlos shook his head, no. "I got kicked out of that school," he said. The principal reminded him that that had happened before he had the skills he has now. He reassured him, "You now know how to handle hard situations and you can regulate yourself. Just try one class. We will pick the class you want to try together." He agreed to try. The principal and Carlos even talked through some challenges he might face and how he would handle them.

Carlos began again at his old high school. After a few weeks he came to see his principal and shared that he was having some troubles with the teacher. The principal said, "You probably know what I am going to say." Carlos said, "Yes. Always talk to the problem not about it. You think I should go talk to my teacher respectfully and see if we can solve it." His principal smiled and supported him by letting him know that he would help with the conversation if he needed help. Carlos said, "No. I got it."

A week passed and the principal got a call from Carlos' teacher at the high school. The teacher was very vague in dialogue, but wanted the principal to know things were good with Carlos and he was enjoying having him in class. Now the principal was confused by the call, so he asked Carlos to come see him. He told Carlos the teacher called and told him things were going well but was a little vague on what had happened. Carlos explained, "I talked to him a couple days ago. I asked to see him after class, and he told me I could come to his office. I told him that I know I'm not your best student and I mess up sometimes, but when you call me out in front of the group it embarrasses me. Last year when a teacher embarrassed me, I did something that got me in lot of trouble. I was wondering if when you think I am messing up, if you could talk with me in your office after class and I will try to change what I am doing wrong."

WOW, what a success story! Taking what he learned and making it transfer to another setting. The principal and school did a lot of spotting of Carlos. The principal knew it was time to increase the weight Carlos would need to lift for himself, but supported him by letting him pick the class, and helped prepare him for the possible challenges he might face. When the challenge arrived, he spotted Carlos with the skills needed but did not do the lifting for him. What a growth Carlos experienced with the spotting of his principal. Carlos graduated and completed the course with a B at his high school.

CONSIDER THIS...

The Problem With Points

Many times, to motivate them, we put children on point systems. Often a student can get so caught up in the points that they fail to connect things back to skill development or their own mastery. When asked about their day, students say, "It was good, I was on blue." If asked, "What does blue mean?" They likely respond, "Good." They rarely relate this back to the schools' foundations and skills. When the teacher assigns points to a color, many student brains will begin to fight for autonomy. A student might say, "My teacher took my points away from me." The brain knows when it is being manipulated, and yes, even a five-year-old brain recognizes this.

Most often point systems encourage students to become manipulative. Kids will say, "I won't do it for one ticket, but I will for two." Or "I don't like oatmeal cookies. Unless you get chocolate chip cookies, I'm not doing it."

Some educators are fearful of moving kids off a points system. They worry they may lose control of the class. A safe first step is to look at which kids need the current system. Often an entire class is on a point system, and many are already doing well and will continue to do so without points. Removing them from the point system could be framed as a positive. "Because you are doing so well, I think it's time for you to do this on your own." Educators can use less supervision for students who demonstrate they can make good decisions. For students who need more support, move them to a self-evaluation process so they can assess their own growth.

PART II

The Responsibility-Centered Discipline Process

CHAPTER THREE

The Foundations

Shifting a School From Rules to Skills (Values)

COMING UP IN THIS CHAPTER . . .

Step 1 in the RCD process:

- **Creating schoolwide foundations**
- **Operationalizing foundations**

Lots of teachers have been trained to start the school year by going over their classroom rules. Most educators themselves have probably had numerous days as a student where they sat in a classroom getting the speech about rules. While, yes, it is helpful to communicate clear expectations, a lot of students begin to tune out. Their first impression of the teacher is that they are controlling and bossy. Widely cited American psychologist Jack Brehm coined the term *reactance* which posits the theory that when a person's freedom is threatened or compromised, they will seek a different action (reactance) to regain it (Brehm, 1966). Therefore, many students' brains become active in the autonomy fight. For some students, this creates a desire to break a few rules just to show the teacher doesn't have control over them. A student may try to fight to regain their autonomy by thinking, "Yeah, just try to get me not to talk in class."

Imagine if during a staff meeting, the school leader said, "Staff, I have a few rules for you that I want to go over. You need to be engaged and focused while we are working in our teams. Your phones need to be off. If you can't do that, you will need to attend without your phone." Pushback would be predictable. Instead, leaders are trained, wisely, to change their language. Rather than using "rules," it's meeting "norms," or "agreements." This may sound like a slight difference in wording, but words and language have power. Some words trigger more of a fight for autonomy response than others. It is time to lead students much more like adults are lead. Adults do not respond well to another adult trying to control them, and many students don't either. This is why the first step in the RCD framework is to create schoolwide goals and move away from traditional rules.

FROM RULES TO SKILLS: CREATING FOUNDATIONS

Schools everywhere display posters with phrases and quotes about doing the right things. They spend time being very explicit with their rules. Some even post the specific rules for every space in the school: the lunchroom, bathrooms, hallways, classrooms, etc. This is a good effort, but when educators begin to think in terms of skills instead of rules, they will have less need for all the detailed lists. Since behavior is a skill, or a lack of skill, school staff should focus on which skills they value most for students. Which ones do they want to commit to building into their students to set them up for ongoing success beyond their school years? RCD refers to these as a school's foundations.

Foundations are what the RCD school is built upon and what drives the daily practices in the building. This process is harder than it appears on the surface and will require strong leadership. This is because it is not just a set of posted rules or the opening speech for the school year. Foundations become a part of everything done within a school.

PRO TIP

Stick to 3–5 skills because too many expectations become no expectations; the brain cannot organize them, and students and staff cannot make sense of them all. Flow charts, matrixes, etc., are too much. Also, foundations should not sound like policies or mission statements.

The first step in creating a school's foundations is to get the entire staff actively involved. Together, the staff agrees on three to five skills that would impact students' lives the most.

The process of building your school's foundations will take some time because it is important to involve everyone in the conversation about which skills would help students reach their goals for future success. Including everyone's input will ensure that the goals reflect the uniqueness of each school community.

ENGAGE STAFF IN CREATING FOUNDATIONS

The following are a few steps to help staff create foundations. A more complete process can be found in Appendix A.

1. Place staff in teams of approximately six to eight and provide them with a large piece of paper to record their ideas.
2. Ask them to brainstorm a list of the current behaviors that are keeping students from doing their best. These are all the behaviors they would like to see disappear.
3. Once lists are generated, reconvene the whole group and allow all participants to review the lists from each team and add or remove content as needed.

The generated lists will likely be filled with things such as not giving best effort, disrespecting peers, incomplete work, cheating, damaging property, arguing with staff, skipping class, bullying, cellphones, vaping, and on and on. Once behavior challenges are agreed upon, it is time to categorize these into the skills students need to tackle these challenges. Staff should consider:

- What are the skills students need to have to eliminate the challenges on the list? For example, if students had the skill of perseverance, then missing assignments or poor effort could be eliminated. Or, if a student was respectful, bullying could come off the list.
- Remember good old character education. Words like, integrity, perseverance, respect, and responsibility are the true skills educators desire. The goal is to think big picture about foundations, rather than just the observed behavior.

PRO TIP

Especially at the elementary level, keep in mind foundational skills such as "safety." Safety is a goal. The skill we desire is a responsible individual who makes safer choices. So rather than focusing on being safe, focus more on the skill of being responsible.

OPERATIONALIZING FOUNDATIONS

Once your foundations are created and agreed upon, it is important to post them in classrooms, hallways, lunchrooms—any place where they are relevant. Utilizing these foundations helps to build a consistency of expectations throughout the school. Everyone can, and should, refer to the poster for help when they are struggling to find the right words while coaching a student through a behavior challenge (more on coaching in Chapter 5). As staff become familiar with the foundations, this becomes automatic. It is also helpful for students to see these clear expectations to help them realize that critical feedback is not personal, but the expectations for everyone in the school. For examples of large colorful posters (which are reproduced in grayscale within this book) celebrating school foundations see Figures 3.1–3.3.

FIGURE 3.1 ● Elementary School Foundations

Perseverance

Try, try, try...Never give up. Always do my best.

Respect

Be kind to myself and others in all I think, do and say.

Integrity

Do the right thing even when no one else is watching. Wrong is wrong even if others are doing it.

Discipline

Think it through before I do. I am in control of myself and my behavior.

Empathy

Understand and respect the feelings of others.

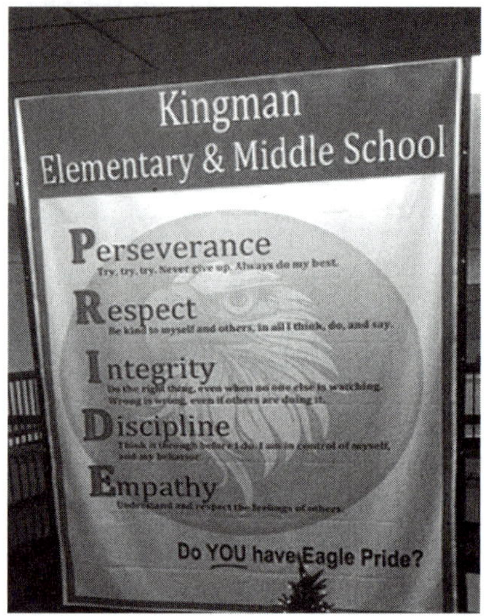

Source: Kingman Elementary Middle School

FIGURE 3.2 ● K-8 School Foundations

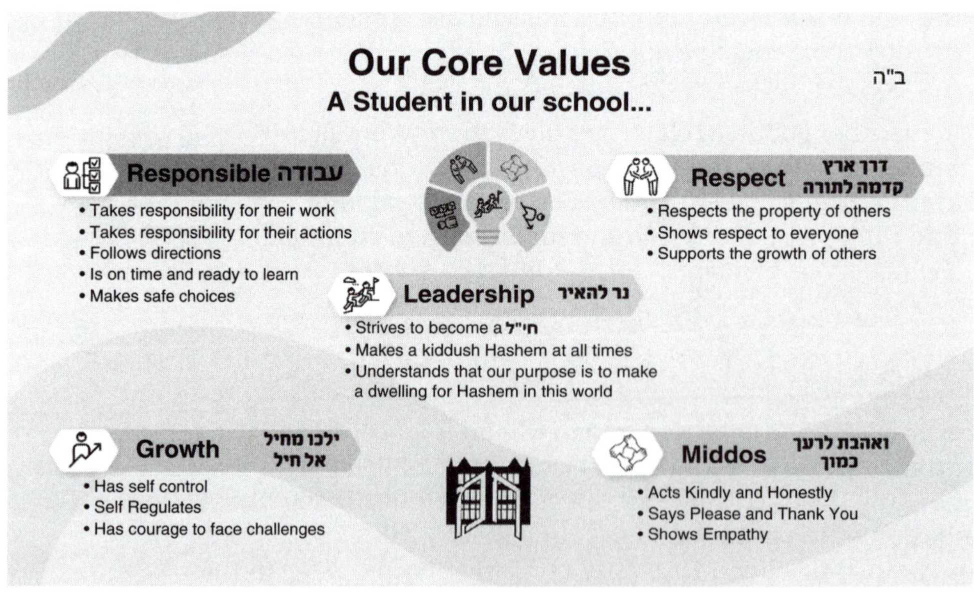

FIGURE 3.3 ● Aberdeen Foundations

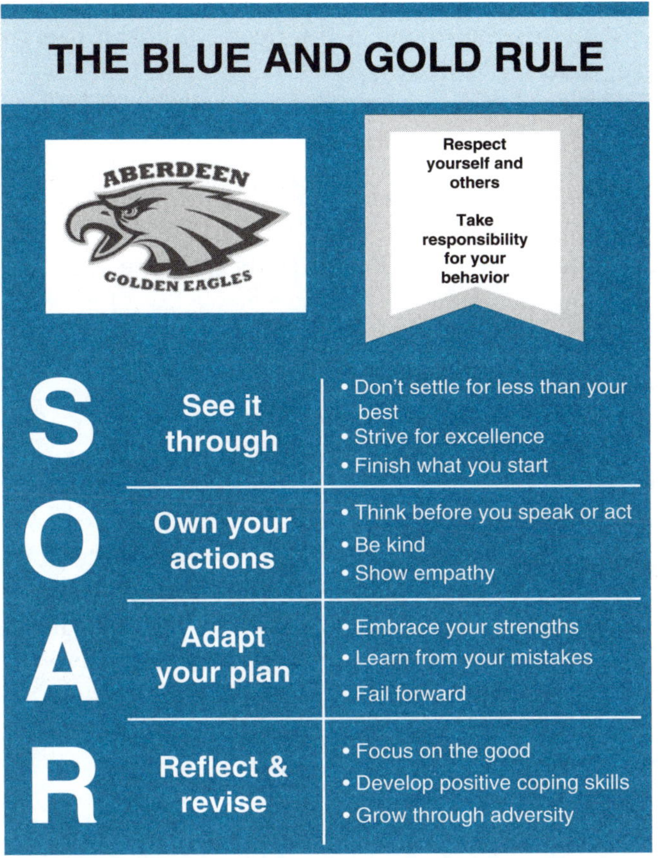

Source: Abereen Golden Eagles

TAKING FOUNDATIONS TO THE STUDENTS

To help students begin to see these foundations as skills, schools need to review them class by class. Educators can begin with a few questions to help students do a little self-assessing on their academic abilities for a specific content area. This will act as a bridge for introducing foundations. For example, a history teacher could ask, "How confident are you in understanding World War II?", an English teacher may ask about the works of an author they will be reading, a physical education teacher may ask about the skill of throwing or catching, etc.

Students write the level of skill or knowledge they think they have right now for each academic skill. "Self-reported grades come out at the top of all influences. Children are the most accurate when predicting how they will perform" (Hattie, 2008). We want students to self-assess both academically and behaviorally, whenever possible.

Self-assessing helps students shift from a fight for autonomy to a focus on mastery. An easy way to self-assess is the 1–4 level used in many schools. Students indicate 1, 2, 3, or 4.

- One means I can't do it yet.
- Two means I can do it with help.
- Three means I've got it on my own.
- Four means I can help others with the skill.

PRO TIP

Frontloading foundations before important events is a good practice. Before a guest speaker comes in, review the relevant foundational skill. If a class is about to review sensitive material, discussing the foundation of empathy is helpful.

To help the shift (from rules to skills) take root in the school community, it is vital for school leaders to set the tone by modeling this language consistently. This is especially important when a student is removed from the classroom. The office should have the foundations posted and the discussion with a student can begin by focusing on the skill that was difficult for them today.

EXPLORE THE BENEFITS OF FOUNDATIONS

After staff have the foundations established, revisit them often. This is a good time to introduce the idea of benefits for the students. Staff can look at the foundations and come up with some benefits for gaining these skills from a student's point of view. Having some benefits in mind will help educators begin to think about how to reply to students who resist embracing the foundations. For example, when a student says, "This is stupid! Why do I have to do this?", the teacher is prepared to speak to the benefit for acquiring a particular foundation.

The benefits are not listed on the foundations posters because each child is different and has their own story. The benefits should be delivered to the student verbally, in a caring manner that best fits their needs. Another way to think about it is the benefits should be in the currency the child carries. Rubles do a vacationer little good when traveling to Mexico. For example:

To help a six-year-old see the benefit of being kind, help them think:

> I will have more friends and people will play with me at recess.

To help a high school student see a benefit of being respectful, help them think:

> I get to be heard when I say it in a respectful way.

THE IMPACT OF A SKILLS FOCUS

When students in RCD schools are interviewed, the message is consistently positive. Figure 3.4 lists a few questions and responses in both an RCD school and a school that has not been trained in RCD.

FIGURE 3.4 • How RCD Students Internalize a Skills Focus

QUESTION	COMMON RESPONSES	RCD RESPONSES
"What does your school value?"	"I don't know" or "Sports"	"Our school foundations." Or they may name specific foundations like "respect."
"What happens at this school when kids are disrespectful?"	"Depends on the teacher."	"Your teacher would talk to you."
"What if you refuse talk to your teacher?"	"You get kicked out of class."	"You may have to get some help working through the problem in the office or solutions area."
"What happens in the office?"	"You have to apologize or get three days ISS."	"You come up with a plan to share with your teacher to show them you are working on the problem so you can get back to class."

These changes may seem small but think about what the students are processing in the RCD replies. The foundations are part of their internal dialog; they have started to internalize the benefits for themselves. Many adults can think of an adult in their childhood who had a major influence on their thinking. The goal is that a school's foundations become a positive inner dialog that will remain with students long after they leave the school building.

Key Takeaways

- Words have power. The word "rules" can activate a student's fight for autonomy.
- Rather than focusing on rules, focus on the skills students need for future success. These will become a school's foundations.
- When creating foundations, involve all staff in identifying specific behavioral challenges.
- Utilizing the foundations provides all students with the tools to grow, not just the more challenging students.
- We must move toward skill development and put the students' brains in the position for growth.
- The goal is for foundations to become an internalized dialog for students.

MEET MRS. THOMPSON

Angela Thompson, my wife, is a former kindergarten teacher. She once had a student on the autism spectrum with a weak self-control muscle. This student who we will refer to as Kaylee, would often lash out with mean and hurtful comments. Mrs. Thompson had many conversations throughout the year with Kaylee where she referred her to the class foundation of kindness and specifically the foundation statement, "If it is not a kind comment, I will keep it to myself." Mrs. Thompson also helped her see the benefit that keeping unkind comments to herself would help her have more friends. One day, Kaylee became frustrated with another student on the playground as she so often did, but this time, rather than lashing out with a stream of hurtful words, she clenched her fists and through clenched teeth said, "If it's not a kind comment I'll keep it to myself!" And she walked away.

- This was a huge moment of growth in this child's muscle of self-control. Had she not heard this foundation message multiple times, she would not have had the internal dialog to coach herself at a moment when she was tempted to lash out. She no longer needed her teacher. The message was within her.

CONSIDER THIS...

Self-Assessment

Just as educators can help students self-assess academically, they can apply this behaviorally. Once students have this framing, it is easier for them to self-assess their strengths in the school's foundations. It can also be helpful for teachers to model these. For example,

> If you overheard someone teasing or making fun of another student, assess your ability to use the foundation of respect.

Level One – The instigator. The one doing the teasing.

Level Two – Laughs but does not get involved.

Level Three – Stays out of it, and does not join in.

Level Four – Stands up for the target and tells the teasers to stop.

Many powerful conversations can happen during this time with students. This is a good time to show that there is often a fine line between responding productively and unproductively. For example, being respectful does not mean a person can't stand up for themselves. Learning how to advocate respectfully is often the challenge.

Self-Assessment for More Challenging Students

Self-assessing is great for all students, but especially for more challenging students. Educators create an individual plan that includes self-assessments to monitor their strength level. If a student needs a more intensive plan for behavior, teachers can set a target skill with them. The target could be staying in their seat, respecting others, or being more responsible with supplies. The teacher keeps a private folder with the chart and the student checks in before leaving to assess how they did. Note, the educator and student must agree on the skill level. This prevents a student from saying they were a four when they were more like a two or vice versa. If students start to ask, "What do I get?", this is their brain thinking about points and rewards. It is better to remind students of the benefits they will receive by acquiring the skill.

Celebrate

Instead of a prize, celebrate the accomplishment with them. Bring snacks to the celebration, but don't make food the focus. The focus should be on the accomplishment. Allow the student to invite someone special to come to the celebration. Make sure this is someone who will be proud of the student and be happy to see their success. Sometimes that may be another teacher, a parent, or a person they know would be proud of their growth. It is powerful for them to have the opportunity to share their mastery.

CHAPTER FOUR

The Six Exits

Recognizing How Students Avoid Responsibility

COMING UP IN THIS CHAPTER . . .

Step 2 in the RCD process:

- **Identifying the Six Exits**

Many years ago, when first hosting RCD trainings, we asked participants to write out things they had heard students say when projecting their problems and avoiding responsibility. This proved to be an easy task since most educators have heard many excuses over the years. They were then asked to come forward and place the sticky note on a life-sized poster of the teacher. This symbolized how students often want to blame the teacher or someone else rather than accept responsibility. Here are a few of the typical responses:

- "I didn't know."
- "She just told me to leave. I don't even know what I did."
- "He was doing it too."
- "Why does it even matter?"
- "She just gets too mad at me."
- "I don't even care. Just give me detention!"

> **PRO TIP**
>
> Keep in mind, when you hear an exit, this is not always an indication that a student is trying to get out of responsibility. It can also be an indication of how the student actually perceives the situation. Either way, it is still important for educators to be able to recognize and coach the student from the exit they are on.

After many years of hearing these types of statements, the Six Exits From Responsibility were identified.

It is important to understand that although students are often on one of these exits, it is the educator's job to close the exits. This requires active listening. Listening to find out which exit the student is on is a skill, and one that will need some coaching. Often, a teacher perceives a student who is unwilling to listen as being defiant. While it may be true that they are being defiant, they are also giving the educator information.

Listening starts with educators challenging themselves to hear what students are saying between the lines in these challenging moments. Skillfully coaching and closing exits requires the educator to first identify which exit is in play.

THE SIX EXITS

1. (No) **Benefit** Exit
2. (No) **Emotional Control** Exit
3. (No) **Clear Expectations** Exit
4. (No) **Consistency** Exit
5. (No) **Leadership in the Moment** Exit
6. (No) **Response-Ability** Exit

#1 THE NO BENEFIT EXIT

Most people don't want to do something for which they cannot see a benefit. Imagine a commercial that advertises a piece of fitness equipment and then closes the commercial by saying it will not make a difference in muscle development. Most would laugh and think, "Why would I ever use that?" So many times, when leading students, educators will fail to understand that they will not join the mission until they can see a benefit. Benefit exit is one of the most common exits off the road to responsibility. When a person does not feel heard and does not feel they have an answer to the benefit question, they often will become more difficult or disengage. This often sounds like continually asking the same question in slightly different ways in an attempt to get an answer. Figure 4.1 shows the difference between dismissive comments versus stating a benefit for the student.

FIGURE 4.1 • Examples of How to Respond to Student Resistance With a Benefit Statement

STUDENT QUESTION	DISMISSIVE ANSWER	RCD BENEFIT STATEMENT
"Why do I even need to do this?"	"Because its required."	"Because this is one of the steps that will make completing your project a lot easier for you."
"It won't make a difference in my grade so why should I do it?"	"My expectation in this room is for you to do your work."	"Perseverance is one of our foundations. I know you're tempted to quit, so let's figure out a way you can push through this and get it done."
"Why can't I be first again?"	"Because we take turns, and it's not your turn to be line leader."	"Everyone enjoys being first. One of our foundations is to be respectful and taking turns is one way we can be fair and respectful of others."

Remember benefits tie back to mastering the foundations (Chapter 3). Utilizing the foundations can make the benefit piece of the conversation easier. The benefits shouldn't be prizes, rewards, or removal of consequences. The benefit needs to be that the foundation is becoming a skill in the student's life.

It is also important to think big when it comes to benefits. Educators generally live in a world that greatly values education and often get stuck making the benefits only academic for students. "You will get a better grade," "You will be more prepared for next year," or "It will help you for college." The challenge is that the benefit must fit the student's life. A benefit for one may not be a benefit for the other. Think of a benefit as needing to be in the currency the child carries. This will help our conversations be real and unique for the different students and situations we are coaching.

PRO TIP

This is where leading staff to think more like students is critical. Ask staff to write age-appropriate benefits for the foundations they collectively created. If respect is a foundation in your school, have each team come up with three benefits for students demonstrating respect in the classroom.

Leading from the benefit helps move the brain out of the autonomy fight and back on the road to responsibility and growth. Remember, teachers may not want to make the changes in discipline if they cannot see the benefits themselves. Coaching from the benefit will help everyone become successful, whether coaching a student or a staff member.

#2 NO CLEAR EXPECTATION EXIT

When an expectation is unclear or unknown, it is very difficult for a person to own their behavior. Being corrected for something not known is downright frustrating. Having very clear expectations leaves less room for confusion and misunderstanding. When this exit presents itself, students respond with comments such as:

- *"I didn't know."*
- *"No one told me."*
- *"It doesn't say that in the handbook."*

Some schools spend countless hours trying to think of every possible misbehavior a student could demonstrate and then create a long list. This is almost helping students find the loophole and live on the exit of unclear expectations. Instead, the foundations are intentionally broad and shared with students often.

Example:

> We will be going to the library and other classes are working or may even be testing. It will be important that we are respectful of the other classes. Please wait until we arrive at the library to talk quietly to each other.

Teachers usually have many opportunities to coach the class or students if the foundation is not being met. Through this process, students begin to understand the foundations holistically. This is better than generating a long list of "what not to do."

PRO TIP

Post foundations throughout the building as a quick reference point for a teacher to use when front loading an expectation or coaching a student. When a student is upset or angry, it can be helpful to direct their attention to the foundations and reteach the clear expectation. When the teacher and student can look together at something instead of looking at each other, it can help get both back on the same page and on the road to responsibility.

#3 NO CONSISTENCY EXIT

Consistency in the RCD process does not mean all situations and students are treated the same. Rather, it means that all students are spotted and given the amount of support needed to get through the challenging moments (Ablon, 2019). Schools have done this academically for years: extra tutoring when a student is struggling, more time to take a test when needed and academic support time built into a school day for help. Many programs train for consistency of the expectations. That is the easy part. RCD focuses first on being sure the expectations are skills, and only then can staff be consistent in coaching when the skill fails to be met.

The following story illustrates the common incident of a student who takes the consistency exit and a teacher who does not have the training to recognize it and coach the student's brain back to growth.

NON-EXAMPLE

The (No) Consistency Exit

Randy was looking at his cell phone when his teacher saw him. Randy knows the expectation is to have phones put away during class.

Teacher:	*Randy put your phone away, you can't have that out while I'm teaching.*
Randy:	*Tina has here phone out.* (Consistency Exit)

Randy is stuck on why this is not consistent, and he cannot process anything else until that question is answered. But this teacher has not been trained to recognize the exit and how to coach it. The teacher responds as most teachers would typically respond:

Teacher:	*I'm not talking to Tina. I'm talking to you.*

So, when this student doesn't feel heard they ask again:

Randy:	*So, Tina gets to do whatever she wants, and I get in trouble?*
Teacher:	*Tina is not your issue; you are responsible for yourself.*
Randy:	*I know you like her better, but really?*
Teacher:	*If you're going to be disrespectful, you can go to the office.*
Randy:	*I am not being disrespectful. I'm just thinking this is not fair.*
Teacher:	*You signed the handbook. You know the rules.*
Randy:	*So did Tina!*
Teacher:	*That's it. Go to the office!*

EXAMPLE

Closing the Consistency Exit

Teacher:	*Randy, please put your cell phone away during class.*
Randy:	*"Tina has her phone out too."*
Teacher:	*"Randy, it is possible that Tina did have her phone out. I may have missed that. I can see where that may even feel unfair to you. It may be a good time for a reminder for the entire class. However, if I say something right now it may be obvious that it's because of our conversation. Could I ask you to trust me that I will address this with the class a bit later?"*
Randy:	*Ok. As long as you will talk to her too!*

By acknowledging Randy's exit, the teacher was able to let him know he was heard. The teacher was able to easily close the exit once she recognized that he was on the consistency exit.

#4 NO LEADING-IN-THE-MOMENT EXIT

Because most college preparatory work did not really prepare educators for challenging moments with students, they often feel unprepared for the disruptions that arise in a classroom. Many educators believe the office is where behavior is coached. They believe the classroom is for teaching, so out the student goes. When a teacher does not lead in the moment and close the exits, the leaders in the office will hear statements such as these from students:

- *"I don't even know why I got sent down here."*
- *"My teacher said if I think it is so funny, I can leave."*
- *"The teacher said they'd had enough of me and told me to come see you."*

Principals often end up in the strange place of not knowing if the child is in "trouble" or just supposed to come see them. RCD is about helping teachers have the confidence to lead in difficult times, to help them be the leaders in these moments. There are additional ways that educators abdicate their leadership during tough moments with students such as sitting a student in the hallway, sending a student to a table in the back of the room, calling a behavior interventionist to talk to the student or even telling the student they are going to call their parent. Another is sending the student to a neighboring classroom. Too often, the student this happens to finds support in the neighboring classroom, and then wants to stay there. Or they disrupt the neighboring classroom which only makes things worse. Educators can become comfortable and confident in leading these moments. This way, the child leaves only for their own lack of skills, not their perception of their teacher's lack of skill. (Situations that involve fights, threats, drugs, or weapons would not be expected to be coached by a teacher but referred to the office right away.)

#5 NO EMOTIONAL CONTROL EXIT

This exit is left wide open for students when the educator loses their emotional control. Most school leaders have heard numerous times from students in the office that they felt mistreated by their teacher. Many teachers resorted in the past to intimidation, embarrassment, and even humiliation of the child to get them to comply. This makes it almost impossible to get a student to assume ownership. Times have changed in our society and most students and parents will not tolerate being treated with disrespect by the adults.

Some educators exclaim that "old school" discipline works. But if that approach worked, it probably was not with a very difficult student. Challenging kids in schools today are not scared of adults. Many are not scared of consequences. To get the student's brain to make a better decision will require closing exits and allowing them, when reregulated, to see the role they played in the situation. An angry teacher doesn't help. In addition, statements such as, "Be the bigger person," "Don't argue with a student," and "Stay calm," are easier said than done. Educators need to practice regulating themselves in these challenging moments so they can avoid leaving the emotional control exit wide open for students. Every time teachers lose emotional control, it not only opens the exit for the student, but also takes a toll on the teacher. Being stressed out all day is a fast route to burnout.

#6 NO RESPONSE-ABILITY EXIT

A key change for most schools transitioning to RCD is no longer allowing time to solve the problems for the students. Educators tend to depend heavily on time to solve the problem for the child instead of relying on the child's brain to solve the problems they create. Think for a moment of all the ways schools have used time over the years to solve the problem for students.

YOUNGER STUDENTS	OLDER STUDENTS
Timeout (x number of minutes/year old)	Thirty-minute detention
Missing 5–10 minutes of recess	Supervised lunch for a week
No leaving the room for drinks until Friday	Three days in ISS

For extreme behaviors, some students may experience leaving the school until next year. All these consequences are about letting the clock solve the problem. These methods are so ingrained in schools that it can be a challenge for leaders to interrupt this habit. This will require a paradigm shift. First, it is important to remember that RCD is not against using time as a part of the consequence, it just cannot be used as a stand-alone. Many feel that if time is not a part of the consequence, educators are being too easy on the kids. Challenging students have learned this system well and often enjoy escaping class. They can be left alone and be done with the work before the rest of the class. Some lack the skills of the foundations and find it easier to go to another place with fewer expectations. If the goal is to move toward students being accountable, leaders must move to accountability for changing the behavior, not accountable for serving the time. More on this in Chapter 7.

Key Takeaways

- Recognizing when a student is exiting responsibility requires the educator to listen to the student to identify which of the six exits the student is on.
- It is important to understand that although students often try to use these exits, it is the educator's job to close the exits.
- Benefit exit is one of most common exits. Many educators fail to understand that students will not join the mission or give full effort until they can see a benefit for themselves.
- The school's foundations are key to communicating clear expectations.
- When an adult is unable to maintain emotional control, an exit is left wide open for students.

MEET MRS. DAVIS

While doing a training in a tough city school, Larry received a great deal of push back from a teacher when sharing that time alone is not an effective consequence. Mrs. Davis challenged, "I don't mean to offend you, but I think you are being too d@#med easy on kids. We are much tougher on kids than you are." She continued, "Students get three days in ISS if they mess up in our school." She was then asked if at the break she could walk us down to see the ISS room. The school had students in attendance that day. I was working with half the staff in the morning and the other half in the afternoon. At the break we walked down, and we stood outside the ISS room and looked through the window of the door. A few students had their heads down and were sleeping. Others were gathered around the teacher's desk talking, while a few were sitting with desks grouped together in the back playing a game. I smiled and said, "Does that look like it's tough for these kids?" She responded with a chuckle, "I guess not." I explained to her that when we let time do the work for the student, it is *easier* for them. And what we are asking for will seem harder for them. When you place time on a consequence it removes the burden for growth and allows something other than the student to do the hard work.

CONSIDER THIS...

When a Student Refuses to Solve a Problem

What if a student refuses to solve the problem? Give it some time and often they will realize this is not a win or lose situation. But in the rare times a student refuses, let them know they cannot continue to fail at this and everything possible will be done to support them. This may mean until they create their own plan, they may need to follow a plan that has been created for them. Example: Student will not stop talking when you are teaching. Move them to a location away from friends who make it tempting to talk. KEY: When they feel they have a strong plan to refrain from talking, remove the temporary plan and allow them to give their plan a try.

CHAPTER FIVE

Closing the Exits

Helping Students Embrace Responsibility

COMING UP IN THIS CHAPTER . . .

Step 3 in the RCD process:

- **The Four Keys for Conversation**
- **Mirror Neurons**
- **Authenticity**
- **The Five-Point Conversation (Give 'em Five)**
- **Improve With Practice**

A skilled coach can teach both beginners and top-level players. Yes, the coaching is different for the specific skills being taught, but the methods of motivating, encouraging, and building self-discipline share many commonalities. Students seldom have the skills to know how to advocate for themselves. However, using RCD, leaders can equip students to acquire the skills to work through struggles with their teachers, which can later transfer to struggles with other students, family, colleagues, and supervisors. Imagine a school where students have the skills to work through hard things with their teachers, peers, and principals. This is possible and can go a long way toward bringing back joy for school educators.

There are three basics to cover before going much deeper into the coaching of challenging behavior:

1. The Four Keys for Conversation
2. Mirroring
3. Authenticity

The second half of this chapter will outline the Five-Point Conversation (Give 'em Five) which makes visible five key aspects for a productive conversation that keeps students on the path of responsibility.

THE FOUR KEYS FOR CONVERSATION

KEY 1: USE THE STUDENT'S NAME WHEN TALKING WITH THEM

This sounds so simple and insignificant, yet the brain has something called relational circuits. These relational circuits show activity when someone calls you by name (Carmody & Lewis, 2006). Relational circuits do not just instantly turn on when the switch is flipped. They take time to warm-up:

> It is important for teachers to make connections with students and establish understanding and trust. Once the relationship is established, it must be maintained by providing regular opportunities for reciprocal communication and positive interactions.
>
> (Cook et al., 2018)

It's not that using a student's name will magically change everything, but it does activate the relational circuits and helps place students in a listening position.

KEY 2: SAFETY FIRST

It is important to remind educators that when they are correcting the student, they are not coaching their own brain, but the student's brain. For example, a child that has experienced abuse or humiliation when an adult has dealt with them in the past may respond differently when the educator gets physically close to them. The key for this is to keep from activating their need for safety through body language and facial expressions. Give the student more space. Sit down, when possible, rather than standing over them and try to assume a relaxed position. Lean back in the chair and be ready to let them talk also. Refrain from pointing at them, crossing arms, and placing hands on hips.

KEY 3: KEEP CONVERSATIONS TWO-WAY

Think in terms of a "sharing conversation" which means students get to speak also (two-way communication is implied in the word conversation, but very often these chats can be quite one-sided). When coaching a very upset student, allowing them to share first can be helpful to give them a voice. Reminder, if a student is not used to this level of respect, it may take them some time to engage.

Also, keep the conversation as private as possible. Going into a hallway is not always necessary; find a moment when other students are busy with a task such as after an assignment is handed out, or when others are packing up at the end of the period.

KEY 4: BE AWARE OF VOICE LEVEL

Educators should keep their voice volume at a level that the student can hear, yet the others in the room cannot. Embarrassment and fear can spark similar responses. When embarrassed, many students escalate, shut down, or walk out as their relational circuits quickly shut off. The goal is for students to mirror the adult. If the educator's voice level is quiet, they are more likely to replicate what they see and hear because of a powerful phenomenon within the human brain called mirror neurons.

MIRROR NEURONS

In a healthy, functioning brain neurons will mirror what they see and begin to feel the emotions and feelings they perceive in the other person. The mirroring is what can cause parents to imitate the movements of a child when watching them play a sport or while watching a favorite team compete. When a parent feeds their baby with a spoon, they often open their mouth when the child should open theirs, even though they are not actually eating. Why? Their mirror neurons are firing (Cattaneo & Rizzolatti, 2009). This is unproblematic in most situations, but if a person begins to mirror someone that is dysregulated and angry, then it can be a recipe for disaster.

Almost every parent and teacher would have to admit they have gotten caught up in dysfunctional mirroring before and usually regret it later. So, to truly master this during challenging moments, it is necessary to practice often with a vigilant eye toward this. Therefore, when the fight, flight, or freeze response kicks in, training can take over and skills can be deployed.

First responders are a great example of this. As they arrive on a scene, they often see horrific and unimaginable things. They too have a fight, flight, or freeze response as all humans do. However, due to their intensive training, they can override their natural response of panic as they think, "This is really terrible!" If first responders can override this automatic response in life and death situations, educators can do the same when a student is determined to run a class off the tracks.

AUTHENTICITY

Picking pre-packaged lines requires little coaching skill and at best only thinly helps address poor student behaviors. Some of the phrases can even sound sarcastic and unsupportive at times. They tend to turn those relational circuits off once again. It doesn't take long before students often start to mimic these same questions and talking points. Imagine, as an adult, if every time a boss called in an employee to discuss a concern it was a script that has already been heard? Adults would not put up with it and neither will most students, especially older ones. A great question to ask when looking at any training from an adult lens is "If this was how I was spoken to would I want to try harder and respect my leader?" If not, it is likely not going to work for students either.

THE FIVE-POINT CONVERSATION (GIVE 'EM FIVE)

The skill used in RCD to help educators support students and build teachers confidence in the challenging moment is a guided five-point conversation called Give 'em Five. Give 'em Five is meant to be interpreted literally as giving five supportive components to students to help them build their problem-solving skills. It is a bold statement of the educator's commitment to offer their students the tools to make change and to be in control of their lives. It is also very easy to recall for educators when they are in the heat of a challenging moment.

The order of the steps may vary because it is important that they do not become rigid scripts that are parroted to students. With enough practice, educators begin to find their own voice and sound like their true selves as they coach student behavior.

Educators use many means to redirect students such as proximity, a quick reminder, a class redirect, or even simply making eye contact with a student. If this takes care of the problem, there is no need to go further. However, educators know far too well this is not always the case. There are times when these attempts do little or nothing to change the students' behavior. When these simple redirects are not effective, an individual conversation with a student may be needed. In a challenging moment, the conversation should contain these five elements:

THE FIVE-POINT (GIVE 'EM FIVE) CONVERSATION

1. Support
2. Expectation
3. Breakdown
4. Benefit
5. Closure

COMPONENT 1: SUPPORT

Support is not a compliment or a catchy cliché, but a genuine way of letting the student know that an educator is on their team and willing to help. Support does not mean the behavior is accepted, and it is important not to send a message that appears to condone wrongdoing. Rather it is supporting the student despite their challenging moment.

Support statements may vary in how they sound. These must be genuine: If a dog knows when you are scared of it, a kid knows when you are full of it. First, look for some positive intent in the negative behavior. For instance, a child who comes racing into class and slides into his seat at the last second, is at least trying to be on time—so let the student hear that, "I appreciate your effort to get to class on time."

Later in the conversation, address the breakdown in how the student entered the room. Another example would be the child who interrupts or forgets to raise his or her hand. The supportive statement could be, "I'm glad to see how excited you are to participate in our discussion." Remember, support must be genuine. Figure 5.1 includes a few illustrative scenarios.

FIGURE 5.1 • Examples of Inauthentic Versus Genuine Supportive Statements

SCENARIO	INAUTHENTIC SUPPORTIVE STATEMENTS	GENUINE SUPPORTIVE STATEMENTS
A student comes running into the room at the last second as the bell rings.	"Well, nice of you to make it to class today."	"Thank you for making an effort to get to class on time today."
A student uses profanity.	"Well, you have a broad vocabulary at least."	"I understand why you are upset."
Student flips off another student.	"That's one way to show off your nail polish."	"Did I miss something? Is anyone being disrespectful to you?"
Student is upset at self for making a mistake and calls themselves stupid.	"I really like your new shirt."	"Try not to be so hard on yourself. Everyone makes mistakes. Including me!"

Source: Olson (2013).

Some examples include:

- "I have seen your best work, and it is excellent."
- "You are a leader, others follow you."
- "When you entered the room today your eyes indicate that your day may not be going so well."
- "Why don't you talk first. There must be more than I know going on."

Support does not have to be first in the conversation. If an educator is too frustrated, it may be best to hold off supportive feedback for the student until later in the conversation. Trying to offer support too soon can easily come across as sarcastic. If sarcasm is used in tough moments, the student will likely mirror it back.

COMPONENT 2: EXPECTATION

Stating an expectation improves clarity about what is expected within the school or the classroom. This would refer to the school foundations posted around the building. It is not necessary to say the word, "expectation," but refer to the skill that the school is working on. Some examples include:

- "One of our school values is that we treat each other with respect."
- "Giving your best effort is hard but we know how important is."
- "Sharing toys is one way we can be a good friend."

Imagine a student who uses language not appropriate for the class and then argues that the language is fine. An educator could remind them that in some settings it may be appropriate, but in the classroom, it is offensive and does not meet the foundational goal of respect. If it offends anyone in this setting, then it does not fit the goal of respect.

COMPONENT 3: BREAKDOWN

The breakdown is all about what went wrong. Sometimes teachers assume the student knows what they did wrong. Often, they do not. A teacher might say, "You know what I need to talk to you about, right?" And the student says something that the teacher was never even aware was happening! So, until both brains are processing the same information, there can be no moving toward responsibility. Including the breakdown in the conversation is important because it assists in being proactive in closing the exit of clear expectations. If the student explicitly knows what she or he did, it makes it less likely to hear the exit statement, "I don't even know what I did wrong!"

Some examples include:

- "I noticed the milk carton missed the trashcan and is on the floor."
- "I am concerned with how hard you threw the ball at Tina."
- "Making noises in class could be distracting and keep others from being able to do their work."
- "I heard you tell Bryson you would not be his friend if he did not let you play with his toy."

COMPONENT 4: BENEFIT

This piece of the conversation is aided by previously completed foundations work from Chapter 2. Reviewing the benefits generated for foundations will help activate them in the challenging moments. This will ward off unnecessarily leaning into traditional consequences or points. Benefits are important because they help move the student out of the autonomy *fight* and back to a focus of mastering the skill. Most educators think they may do parts of this five-point conversation already. However, they find that the benefit piece of the conversation is a new way of thinking and often is the most challenging of the five. This part of the conversation will require practice to come up with strong benefits for the student. Educators or parents who work with young students know all too well the "Why?" question asked often as young children try to make sense of the world. The benefit piece is an answer to that "why" question. The benefit helps students begin to understand why they are being asked to do something which often helps to bring down their defenses.

Some examples include:

- "Being honest and telling the truth can make it more likely that you will have more friends."
- "If you use your class time to work on your assignment, I can help you if you need any help."
- "When I know I can trust you I can say yes to you more often."
- "When you share your opinions respectfully you are more likely to be heard."

COMPONENT 5: CLOSURE

Closure is the sense that things have progressed enough for the educator and the student to move ahead, and the issue is resolved. This does not mean the student says, "Thanks for the feedback. I'm really growing in your class!", but more that the conversation can finish up and the student and educator can move forward. Closure is an important step because if either person walks away without things resolved, the issue has an increased chance of rearing its head again in a very short period of time. The goal is to begin to model for students that in healthy relationships there can be hard moments, but when both people try to communicate, they can have healthy closure.

Some examples include:

- "I'm happy to help you get started if you need help."
- "Does that make sense to you?"
- "Do you think you can work on this?"
- "I know you've got this!" (possibly with a fist bump)
- "Thanks for being so respectful while we talked."

The following is a non-example and an example of a good Give 'em Five.

NON-EXAMPLE

Ms. Haskel noticed one of her middle school students, Jackson, had not turned in an assignment for the past three days. Jackson does not use his class time to work on the late assignment but instead talks to friends. Ms. Haskel decided to address this behavior today and attempted to use her new skills in Give 'em Five. She went to Jackson in the back of the room and told him he needs to give his best effort. She reminds him that best effort is a schoolwide expectation. She shared that grades improve when you try hard and give your best effort. She leaves the conversation by telling Jackson "You're better than this." As Ms. Haskel walked away, Jackson rolled his eyes at her behind her back.

What's Missing

Although Ms. Haskel did name the expectation of giving best effort, she failed to clearly identify the breakdown or exactly where Jackson's behavior was not meeting the standard. When the breakdown is not clearly communicated, it leaves the door open for the student to dismiss the conversation or even at times be confused of why the teacher even talked to them. Ms. Haskel did not include support statements in the conversation. She did include the benefit of improved grades from giving best effort. However, educators know that some students are more motivated by grades than others. She may have thought her comment "You're better than this" was closure. However, by saying this to him she triggered his fight for autonomy, which likely was the reason for the eye roll.

EXAMPLE

Jackson, I know this is not your favorite subject. You've shared that with me before. It is hard to get ourselves to do things we do not want to do (Support). For the past three days you have told me you would turn in the assignment. I have given you class time to work on catching up and you are spending the time talking. Talking instead of working isn't giving your best effort (Breakdown). One of our classroom and school goals is giving our best effort (Expectation). When you use your class time to work hard on your assignment, not only are you more likely to get it done and turned in on time for full credit, but I am also here to help you if you have any questions (Benefit). If you are needing any help understanding the assignment or getting started, I am more than happy to help you get going (Closure).

The five-point conversation gives educators a skill that can be practiced together. Because it is skills-based, progress can be measured with specific feedback about which parts of the conversation are missing or inadequate. This is how educators' confidence can grow in this area.

These conversations help educators remain in a coaching role with behavior and avoid the temptation to lose control or relinquish authority.

PRO TIP

When a school's staff begins to really work on the skills of coaching challenging behaviors, they will soon realize how differentiated the process becomes. Some teachers may need Give 'em Five to help with their own emotional control while another teacher needs it to gain confidence in correcting behaviors. Both the "over" and "under" spotting staff can benefit from something they can practice to begin mastering the challenging moments.

PRACTICE AS A TEAM

RCD breaks student challenging moments into three levels of intensity:

INTENSITY LEVEL ONE

The student quickly recognizes that he/she has made a mistake, takes responsibility for the problem, and works well with the teacher to resolve the issue.

INTENSITY LEVEL TWO

The student begins to display signs of unwillingness to accept responsibility—including arguing, denying, ignoring the teacher, crying, interrupting, etc. At this stage, the educator begins hearing the exits student may take from responsibility (see preceding chapter). The educator must use additional strategies to coach and redirect the student. Though the student offers more resistance at this level, with coaching closure is achieved.

INTENSITY LEVEL THREE

> The student is unable to maintain self-control and refuses to accept responsibility. The student is unable or unwilling to work through the process with the teacher. Despite the educator's skillful coaching, closure is not achieved, and the student is referred for more support. More on these students in the next chapter.

PRO TIP

When first beginning role-playing with staff, provide written scenarios. Choose scenarios that commonly occur in your building. Providing scenarios at first saves time. Eventually, allow your staff to bring situations they are encountering in their own classrooms to keep practice relevant for them.

When facilitating professional development with staff, start all educators off with level one challenges so they can experience success. Once all staff are confident with level one challenges, then move to levels two and three. Practice must feel safe for teachers. This is where it is recommended having staff write out a scenario with their conversations. Then, have them share the first one and discuss with a colleague. The second written one they would write and then do a role rehearsal of the actual scene with a partner. The third written one is timed to encourage them to think quickly on how they might structure the conversation.

Sample Level 1 Conversation

(additional examples in Appendix B)

Teacher:	Kendra, thank you for coming over here to talk with me. I know you are having fun playing (Support). I could see you allowing some kids to go on the slide and telling others they could not go down today (Breakdown).
Kendra:	Yeah, if they do not know the password they can't go down.
Teacher:	At recess we want everyone to have fun and have a chance to use all the equipment (Expectation). Even though it may be fun for you, I don't think it is as much fun for kids who do not know the password. You told me the other day that you are hoping to make some new friends this year. Letting everyone play will make that more likely (Benefit).
Kendra:	I do want to make new friends.
Teacher:	Super! We still have a few more minutes to play. Make sure you allow everyone to play on the slide. Now, go have fun! (Closure)

After everyone feels comfortable writing a five-point conversation, they can begin practicing in a larger group. Appendix B includes a step-by-step process that has more detail on facilitating this process.

Key Takeaways

- Becoming highly skilled in the challenging moments requires training that simulates the stress of the moment.
- The skill used in RCD to help educators support students is a guided five-point conversation called Give 'em Five: Support, Expectation, Breakdown, Benefit, Closure.
- This guided conversation closes the exits students try to take.
- Good conversations include the educator modeling active listening, self-regulation, and authenticity.
- Learn to identify the three levels of student behavior:
    - Level 1: Student takes responsibility and works well with the teacher to resolve the issue.
    - Level 2: Student shows signs of struggling to accept responsibility, additional strategies for coaching are needed to achieve closure but closure is reached.
    - Level 3: Student is unable to maintain self-control and refuses to accept responsibility. Closure is not reached despite educators skillful coaching.

MEET OUR DAUGHTER

Many years ago, when one of our daughters was about four years old, we were noticing that when she got frustrated or upset, she would become very loud and very verbal. As a young dad, I would try to talk to her, but I was not able to get her to listen. My wife, who was a kindergarten teacher said, "Larry, when she gets that upset, she is not going to hear anything you have to say to her. You just need to give her some time." So, the next time she became very upset, I remembered my wife's advice. I looked around and saw a stack of carpet samples from our home remodel project. I quickly grabbed three and laid them out in the hallway. I explained to her, "Daddy is going to have you start out here on the first mat. You can stay there if you need to or as long as you are feeling sad or mad." I then told her, "Once you are feeling better you can move to the middle mat to think. When you are on the middle mat, think about what happened. Think about why you got so upset. Then think about how we can fix this problem." I then told her, "When you are ready to talk to daddy, sit on this last mat here." She sat down on the first mat, clearly still highly emotional. After a few minutes passed, I glanced in the hall to notice she was now sitting on the middle carpet sample. She was visibly calmer. She had stopped crying loudly and appeared to be looking straight ahead and deep in thought. A few minutes later she was sitting on the last mat. When we made eye contact. I even noticed a slight smile on her face. (I now understand she was proud of herself—this was a mastery moment for her) We talked about what happened and ended our conversation with a hug. I was pleasantly surprised at how well this worked.

A few weeks later while working at a local elementary school a student came into the office very upset and dysregulated. The principal informed me this happened frequently with this student, and he asked me, "What would you do in this situation?" Recalling the previous interaction with my daughter, I noticed three chairs in his office: a red, a yellow, and a blue. I said, "Have him sit in the red chair while he is still too upset to talk. Then have him move to the yellow when he is ready to think. Tell him when he is sitting in the blue chair you will know he is ready to talk to you." Once again, it worked!

After years of experience and learning, it is now understood why this worked so well. It is the process of self-regulation. Self-regulation is an abstract concept. Many children learn this through it being modeled in the home. Unfortunately, this is not modeled in all homes. Many adults still do not have this skill. Out of personal experience, the Response Ability mats were created to teach young children the process of self-regulation. More on the mats can be found in Appendix C.

CONSIDER THIS...

Finding the Balance

To prepare educators for the higher-level challenges, support must move at an appropriate and realistic pace. Picture a seesaw. On one side of the seesaw is skill level and the other side is stress level (see Figure 5.2). When we learn a new skill, the skill level is weak. When a skill is weak, stress levels tend to increase (Olson, 2013). But as the skill improves, the stress level comes down. Leaders of schools need to help shift the balance for educators so that they can eventually experience success.

FIGURE 5.2 ● The Seesaw Effect of Skill Acquisition

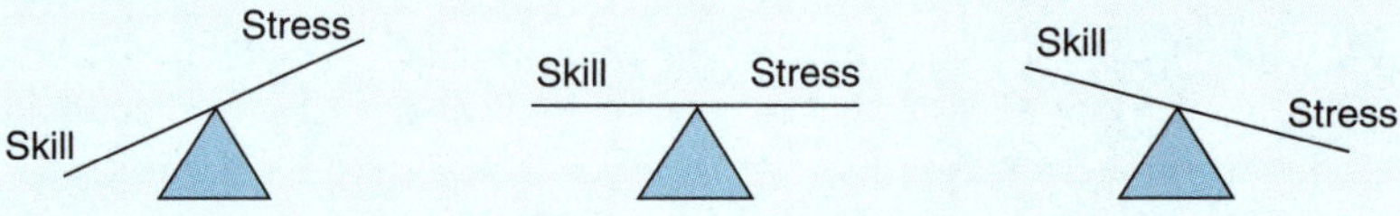

The first step in the practice process is to assure all staff are skilled in a level one five-point conversation (where a student realized they made a mistake and closure happens quickly). Once the staff feels ready to move to a tougher challenge level, begin to increase the difficulty. (Allow staff to self-report when they are ready for the next level of challenge.) A level two student begins to take exits and challenge the teacher and a level three is a student you cannot redirect despite strong teacher skills, so office support is needed.

There are no shortcuts for this; lots of repetition and practice are necessary.

CHAPTER SIX

Addressing Higher Levels of Challenge

Assisting Students Who Need More Support

COMING UP IN THIS CHAPTER . . .

Step 4, Part I in the RCD process:

- **Using support and benefits statements to:**
  - **help students stay in the classroom**
  - **close the exits**
  - **provide attunement**
- **Pausing a challenging moment**

The last part of the RCD process is creating a solutions space which is needed when a student must be removed from the classroom to work on their behavioral skills (level three intensity). However, there is a lot that happens in the moments before an educator makes this decision. To capture this complexity, the solutions part of the RCD process is broken into two sections: what happens during the moments when a student is at high risk for being sent to the office (Part 1, Chapter 6) and what happens when a student is sent to the office (Part II, Chapter 7.

If a challenging moment has risen to the level that an educator is considering sending a student out of the classroom, then it is fair to assume that tensions are running high for both the student and the teacher. The best way to begin is to have staff rehearse the following skills often so their judgment remains strong when a situation is approaching a level three intensity.

LEANING INTO SUPPORTS AND BENEFITS

When a student continues to struggle through the five-point conversation, educators should switch to only two of the five: **support** and **benefit**. These are two of the harder parts of the conversation and will take coaching and practice. When student behaviors begin to escalate, it is common for teachers to begin to mirror the student's negative behaviors. They get louder as the student gets louder. As the student demonstrates more posturing, the teacher does as well. The teacher may even resort to threats to stop the misbehavior. This is why it is important to help staff attune with the student and begin to mirror their own self-regulation. Attuning is described as alignment to another, congruency, or being "in-step" with someone (Siegel, 2007).

Attuning is a little like a tennis volley. The student serves over some anger, but the teacher responds with a benefit and support. By doing this, they allow students to borrow their emotional control when the student cannot find their own. Figure 6.1 includes a few examples of the difference between a traditional response versus a Responsibility-Centered Discipline response using supports and benefits.

FIGURE 6.1 • Traditional Response Versus an RCD Response Using Supports and Benefits

SCENARIO	TRADITIONAL SCHOOL RESPONSE	RCD SCHOOL RESPONSE
Student: "Leave me the F@#& alone!"	"You are not going to use that language in this class!"	(Support) "I am trying to hear you, (Benefit) "The F word makes it hard to really hear what you mean. Can you tell me without that?""
Student. "I am never going to need any of this in my life so I'm not doing it."	"You will use this when you get a job, and my expectation is for you to work, or you will not get the credit."	(Support) "Let's set the assignment aside for a moment. To be honest, I am not 100% sure you will use it. (Benefit) I do know you will have to

		persevere in your life. When we don't want to do something is when we must really rely on our perseverance. So, don't give up. You are stronger than you think."
Student: Hides when asked to come speak to you.	"I see you hiding. Get out of there and come over here and talk to me."	(Support) "I'm not sure if you are hiding because you are scared? I just want to talk with you. (Benefit) I want to make sure you are safe in the hallways."

PRO TIP

People often ask if there is a set number of supports and benefits. There is not. But once an educator realizes a student appears to be getting further away from working with them, even after supports and benefits, the next progression is to switch to giving the student's brain some time.

MORE ON PAUSING FOR MASTERY

This concept was introduced in Chapter 2, and it is showing up again because of the impact it can have on students approaching a level three.

The key when offering time is not to talk down to the student or shame them for the struggle. Imagine spouses or significant others having an argument. Picture if one said, "I can see you need a minute." The other person will likely not feel they are being supported and may even say, "No! What I would like is for you to ___________."

Another common response is asking the student if they would like some time. This can work with some students, but often an escalated student will not respond with, "Yes, please," but "No! What I need is for you to leave me alone!" Instead ask educators to think of three ways they could encourage students to take some time, or put things on pause, for the child. Encourage educators to do so without the student even realizing what's happening to avoid coming across as condescending. Once given the time, leave students with a support statement.

Some examples of supportive time statements include:

- *"I need to get the class started. When I come back, we can figure this out. We did last time."*
- *"I need to take attendance, then I can check back in with you. I will be fair with you."*

PRO TIP

Be careful about asking a dysregulated student to go to a hallway or get a drink. Often a bigger problem can develop if someone approaches them in that space.

After you have given the brain a little time to reregulate, move back in and continue the process with them—but check their body language first.

- *"I am going to go check on this group. Then I will be back so we can finish chatting. I'm sure we can quickly wrap things up so you can get back to your project. I see how much you're enjoying it."*

It is important to understand that educators cannot force a student to take some time. If they continue to disrupt the class, move to the next progression more quickly. When the student is reregulated in the office, they should be reminded of the teacher's attempt to give them time to work through the situation. This will help the student move closer to accepting time in the classroom the next time it is offered.

BEYOND SUPPORT AND BENEFITS

When time or pausing is not helpful for the student, it is time to move to the next level. This is one more effort to try to support the student.

This is a challenge for teachers, and by the time they are at this progression, their level of frustration might be on the rise. This is when a teacher must communicate to the student that they would like to help them resolve the situation but if they are not able to do so, it will require additional help and support from the office. This is when the student will need to make a decision: Are they going to choose to work with the educator, or will they need to leave the room?

PRO TIP

Some of our most challenging students may need intensive spotting as the muscle of self-control is weak. Students with trauma and emotional challenges will need spotting in ways that our training in trauma and special education are aligned. Educators need to be trained in how to understand and recognize children in trauma.

ONE MORE ATTEMPT TO KEEP STUDENTS IN THE CLASSROOM

If a student who is fighting for autonomy perceives a threat this often will escalate the behavior. It is critical for educators to communicate in a nonthreatening manner. Figure 6.2 shows the distinction between productive and unproductive statements.

FIGURE 6.2 • Productive Versus Unproductive Statements

TRADITIONAL SCHOOL RESPONSE	RCD SCHOOL RESPONSE
"Keep it up and see what happens. . ."	"I know you have a game later and you don't want to get on that bus worrying about a school issue. I want to try to resolve this one more time. Will you work with me?"

"If you're going to keep acting like this, you may need to go to the office!"	"We don't need to make this bigger than it is. Let's both try it again with our focus being on respect and see if we can get it figured out."
"This is your office referral warning!"	"The class needs me. We need to decide now if we can try one more time to work together to figure this out without needing more support from the office."

SENDING A STUDENT TO THE OFFICE

Once another chance has been given, it is important that the student knows that this means they are referred out of class for more support. This is the window they must decide whether they want to go down to a level one and stay in class or move to a level three and be sent to the office. If the student is unable to resolve the problem with the educator's help, the educator still has a responsibility to communicate effectively in a supportive manner to let the student know this will require more help than can be provided in the classroom at this time. Figure 6.3 compares traditional office referrals being issued versus RCD statements.

Because closure is not achieved in the classroom with a level three, when a student is referred to the office, closure will be addressed upon the student returning. Chapter 7 will go into the details of what happens while the student is out of the classroom.

PRO TIP

At this stage in the conversation a teacher may feel frustrated and unintentionally leave exits open for the student. The last words a student hears before leaving the room are important. Remember the student is leaving due to their lack of skill. So, this must be stated as a skill.

FIGURE 6.3 • Traditional Office Referrals Versus RCD Statements

TRADITIONAL SCHOOL RESPONSE	RCD SCHOOL RESPONSE
"Go to the office."	"I can see we are not able to get this resolved together, so I will have you get further support in the office."
"You've just earned an office referral."	"I am going to have you get more help in the office."
"If you think this is so funny you can see how funny it is in the office."	"I am disappointed we couldn't resolve this. I will have you get more help in the office."

SUGGESTIONS FOR TEACHER PRACTICE

These new skills will likely be a learning curve for educators. Therefore, pacing is everything. Do not role play a level three student when the initial practice called for simulating lower-level challenges. Staff need time to self-assess and share their readiness levels. Remind them that student growth will be directly related to all staffs' skill development. Once all staff are highly skilled in coaching with fidelity, and the solutions process is in place, general accountability will shift to the students. Educators will move from coaching student behavior from an autonomy perspective to a mastery perspective which will decrease their stress. Why? If teachers coach from autonomy, they will be angry when they can't get control of the student. When they coach from mastery, the teacher is disappointed when the student does not accept the help.

Key Takeaways

- When learning to deal with a student on or approaching a level three, teachers will likely be weak in this skill at first. They will need support and training to build their confidence.
- When students escalate to levels two and three, educators should focus on the support and benefit aspects of the five-point conversation.
- Educators should look for an opportunity to pause the moment to help a student self-regulate.
- If the student must leave the room, it is important that the educator is supportive and nonthreatening when communicating this.
- Student growth is directly related to all staffs' skill development. Once all staff are coaching with fidelity, accountability will shift to the students.

The following story comes from an RCD leader at a large school. To respect the privacy of the student, they/them pronouns are used, and some details have been changed.

MEET THE LATE STUDENT

Late into the school year during our first year implementing Responsibility-Centered Discipline, I received an office referral for a student. This student had suddenly started to be habitually late to class and demonstrated apathy when the teacher addressed the concern. When their name came across my desk, I was perplexed as it was not a name I was familiar with. I did a quick search for their name in our school database system and learned they were in their first year at our school. They did not have a disciplinary record and there were no concerns highlighted from previous school districts.

With that information in hand, I set out to speak with the teacher. "So tell me about this student, I don't know them yet." The teacher immediately replied, "I did Give 'em Five each time they were late." I responded, "Great! What did it sound like and how did they respond?" The teacher highlighted the foundation of accountability and went through the Give 'em Five conversation. Being new to the RCD philosophy and not experienced yet with a level 3 behavior, I felt like the teacher did an outstanding job. The teacher then said, "It seemed like no matter what I said they didn't care and even responded, 'Write me up then!'" I assured the teacher that we would work together to find some solutions that may work.

At this point they were in the hallway with me, and I attempted to talk to them. They were defiant and said several times, "Just send me home, I don't care." I told them at our school we work through hard things together and that if they were not ready to talk with me, they could get some help in the solutions room. They fired back. "What is a solutions room?" I told them it is a place to work through a problem with people who could help. They again said, "Take me home. At my old school when I got in trouble, they sent me home." I replied, "We used to do that too, but now our school solves problems and we will help you." I knew that we needed to find some common ground and that I would have to use my benefit and support statements. I used several supports and benefits as their anger was directed toward me. At one point, our resource officer asked if I wanted help. But I was not ready to give up. They finally agreed to go to the solutions room with me and when I walked them into the solutions room, they greeted the educators working in that room with, "I'm not talking to either one of you." They replied, "You don't have to until you're ready." They too were highly skilled at spotting students. These educators were some of our best with RCD. In a few hours, I had a call that they were ready to talk.

I welcomed them into my office and introduced myself. They took a seat and slouched sideways. I explained to them that the teacher had created a disciplinary referral for them being late to class. They again stated that at their old school they would have just assigned a consequence. I replied, "At this school we work through our problems." They did not like this response and became obviously agitated. They expressed to me clearly using profanity that they didn't care, so I should just give them a consequence and they were not going to get better no matter what. I knew at that moment that to help them, I needed to fill my conversation with support. Needing more time to process myself, we sat in silence for a few minutes. Ready to move forward with the conversation, I sat back into my chair and said, "I am confused." They responded, "What do you mean?" I said, "I don't understand how you are a student with decent grades, no attendance issues, you've never been in my office before, and suddenly you are going down this path. What has changed?" They paused, then said to me, "You wouldn't understand." I assured them that I may not understand but at least we could have open communication regarding what was going on. They immediately said, "I have new friends." My years of experience working with middle school aged youth, I understood that it is not uncommon for peer issues to be the center of discipline struggles at school. I said, "Ok, is this a good thing or bad thing?" They said "Well, at the moment it is a good thing." I really was not sure what they meant by that. I asked them to tell me more. At that point, they sat up in their chair and said "Well, the new friends are the only ones accepting of me right now." I said, "It's great that you have friends that are being good to you. What does that have to do with you being late for class?" The student then said, "I tried to kill myself last week and my old friends will not be friends with me anymore. But my new ones are making poor decisions, and I am following along. I don't know what to do. I don't want to not have any friends. So, I thought even bad friends are better than no friends." They began to cry and said, "But now I don't know what to do!" At this point they were sobbing uncontrollably. I handed them a tissue and told them you have as much time as you need in here. After a few minutes, they looked up through bloodshot eyes and said, "Mr. H. thank you for not sending me home today. My parents are gone, and I have been planning to take my life."

Now we both were in tears, and I just supported them and told them I am so glad we solve problems at this school. We got the proper supports into their life and communicated with their family to keep them safe. They received the help needed, and things greatly improved. They had a good school year and sadly to me, moved to another town for high school. They continued to stay in touch, and I received letters from them about their continued progress.

Following this event, I called my friend, Larry Thompson, to share my experience with him. After sharing what happened, I told him, "Larry, if I had sent them home, as we may have in years past . . . I just can't even imagine how I'd live with myself if they had followed through on their plan." I'm grateful RCD is changing our school to solve problems.

CONSIDER THIS...

Calibrating the Office Referral

When spending time around school administrators, it does not take long before frustrations are heard regarding office referrals. When administrators are asked the question, "What percentage of students are sent to the office who you believe did not need to be sent?" In most schools, the numbers range from 50% to higher. So, at best, half of all referrals were unwarranted according to these school leaders.

Principals are trying to get things done and then they are interrupted with a call letting them know a student is on the way to the office. In most schools, the principal listens to the student for a while. Seldom is the student taking ownership for the mistake. Most often they are on one of the six exits. Depending on the school, the principal may send the kid to in-school-suspension or give some sort of pep talk about life and then return them to the room hoping things will get better. Overtime, however, reality starts to take hold. Principals realize if the student is sent back to the teacher's classroom and they act up again, the teacher will be mad at them also.

When teams begin to measure behaviors consistently, most should come to the same conclusion about level one versus level three scenarios. When this consistency is achieved, the administration and teachers become a team and the frustrations with one another regarding the office referral rapidly decrease. This is what will prevent the Bermuda Triangle effect from happening in schools.

GUIDANCE FOR CALIBRATING OFFICE REFERRALS

1. All classrooms use the foundations as the standards for the expectation and the behavior.
2. Clear expectations are communicated to the staff regarding what an office referral is: a student leaves the classroom for safety issues or if they are unable to receive the coaching from the teacher.
3. Through quality practice, staff will move through the levels of challenging behavior and become consistent and recognize when the referral should occur.
4. Leadership oversees implementation by supporting staff and ensuring fidelity of the referral process.

CHAPTER SEVEN

In-School-Solutions

Reimaging School-Based Suspensions

COMING UP IN THIS CHAPTER . . .

Step 4, Part II in the RCD process:

- **Creating a solutions space**
- **Monitoring a solutions space**
- **The referral process**

For too long, schools have allowed something other than the student to solve the problem—the clock. Young children are told, "Ten minutes out of recess," "Lunch at the supervised table until Friday," or "No getting drinks the rest of the day." With older students, it's, "You have a lunch detention," "You are in In School Suspension for the next three days," or "You are expelled for one school year." Think of adding to the end of each of these statements, ". . . then your problem will go away." This sounds silly, but this is what is communicated to students. No matter the severity of the behavior, the clock is doing the work, not the child. Anything that solves the problem other than the student is not really solving the problem.

Placing timeframes on a consequence also implies that there is no action that a student needs to take. This unintentionally removes the growth from the child and robs them of a mastery moment. Instead, educators must realize that time does not solve problems, people do. With this new approach, the goal is no longer accountability for the consequence ("I was in detention for lunch") but accountability for changing the behavior ("I thought of a way to manage my anger"). Keep in mind, that time consequences are not inherently wrong, but they must be coupled with the student solving the problem. When EdSource interviewed Daniel Losen, director of the Center for Civil Rights Remedies at UCLA's Civil Rights Project which analyzes racial inequities in public education, he had this to say, "The goal should be to get to the root of the problem and get kids back in class as soon as possible. What's counterproductive is if kids are sent to sit in a room with someone who's just there to babysit and they're not getting any support" (Jones, 2019). Chapter 7 details the last part of the RCD framework, with a specific focus on In School Suspension (ISS) rooms.

IMPROVING OUT-OF-CLASS DISCIPLINE PRACTICES

Schools should move away from ISS standing for "in-school-suspension" and instead move to an ISS that stands for "in-school-solutions." The acronym ISS can still be used, but the meaning and purpose of the strategy is very different. The in-school-solutions room should be a place to work on improving behavior. The goal of this room is to open the heuristic process in the student's brain to help them find their own novel way to conquer the challenge they are having. When a student is referred from class, they go to the *solutions* room for support and coaching (Figure 7.1).

FIGURE 7.1 • Traditional School Consequence Versus RCD Consequence

TRADITIONAL SCHOOL CONSEQUENCE:	RCD CONSEQUENCE:
"You will serve three days in ISS for disrespecting your teacher."	"You were asked to leave class for being disrespectful to your teacher. After talking with your teacher, it appears he really tried to help you. I can even share what he did to support you. In order to return to class, you'll need to have some ideas for how to work through things in a more respectful manner the next time."

THE SPACE

Before getting into the procedures, it is important to take care of a few basics. This room is best if located away from a major traffic area in the school. This is not a place for students to feel shamed or on display. Therefore, a location with few distractions is best. The room should not be overly comfortable, nor should it be more inviting than the classroom. It should not feel like a reward to hang out in this space. Conversely, this space should not be a place that has miserable conditions in effort to make it feel like punishment. Often schools use cubicles or dividers to help kids maintain a bit of privacy, so they can work on solving their problems free from others listening in. (This does not serve the same purpose as a sensory room, which some schools do have. The sensory room is a better fit to assist some students who are dysregulated before their brain is ready to work on a solution.)

THE STAFF MEMBER

Staffing this position takes some thought. Because this is an important component of RCD implementation, this needs to be a person who is trained and skilled to provide the right balance for spotting of students. They do not over spot and do too much of the work for the student, but they have good relationships and are a strong mentor. This person must be seen as a person who students believe will listen to their side of things; a supportive adult who is in their corner and believes in them. This adult cannot solve their problem, but they will walk alongside the student as they figure it out. It is not uncommon to find students who no longer struggle with behaviors in the school, continue to stop by and share their mastery moments with this individual.

PRO TIP

When looking for the right people in your school to oversee the in-school solutions room, it is important that students respect and trust these people. Who do kids ask for when they're in distress? Who do they listen to, even when being given feedback? Which adult is regularly willing to help with a student? Which adult is able to attune and support even when students are highly agitated? Most staff can readily identify these people.

COMMUNICATION

In our larger schools with multiple principals, this process can actually save school leaders time. Once the solutions room is running with fidelity, the school leader will not be involved again until the solutions staff member notifies them that the student is ready with a solid plan. At this point, the leader assesses whether the plan is appropriate, and then the student is brought back to the classroom to share their plan with the teacher.

Will most students enter the solutions room eager to do the work? Probably not. But remember many schools require up to three days of sitting, and in training many schools with RCD, most students do not sit that long before they are willing to work on the behavior. And the better the coaching and closing of the exits is by the educator, the more willing a student is to see their mistake.

NO ASSIGNMENTS

While in the solutions room, students do not do academic work. In traditional ISS, students are used to getting their assignments and doing them in the ISS room. This should be changed for three reasons:

1. Teachers do not really have the time to gather the correct work and often must give the student something different than what the class is doing also known as busy work.
2. The student begins to see less value in the teacher and just thinks they need the assignments.
3. Students are not getting the same level of teaching and learning when they are out of the classroom.

Shifting to a solutions room decreases loss of future instructional time for many students. Without this reframing, students are sent back to the classroom without a real plan for a change, and the behavior likely will happen again. When it happens another time, the consequence is usually more severe. This is how problems compound for a student, and it becomes much harder for them to reverse course. Instead, schools should provide missed work and offer it as homework. The student can even check with the teacher for help before leaving for the day.

THE REFERRAL PROCESS

No more asking teachers to write office referrals. When a teacher has given a student a five-point conversation, multiple supportive statements, shared the benefits of changing their behavior, offered pausing the moment and the student is still unable to work through the problem, it is time for them to go to the office for further support. The last thing the teacher should have to do is go to the computer and write a referral. The teacher must focus on getting the class back to learning as quickly as possible. It is important for the learning to resume, and for other students to realize their teacher is not shaken by the problem. Students need to see that one student's disruption does not need to affect the rest of the class.

THE BIG PICTURE: THE OFFICE REFERRAL STEPS

To provide the overall picture, here are the general steps for the office referral process. See Appendix E for more details.

STEPS FOR THE OFFICE REFERRAL PROCESS

1. The referring educator communicates that a student needs more support than can be provided in the classroom.
2. The school leader gets the student situated in a safe space. (office or solutions room)
3. The school leader records basic information on referral form (see sample in Appendix D).
4. The school leader goes directly to speak to the person who referred the student to gather basic information regarding the incident and the five-point conversation.
5. The school leader records referring educator's support and benefit statements, and if a pause was offered. (This is critical so the school leader or solutions room leader can show the student that they are aware of how they were supported in the classroom.)
6. School leader asks referring educator how strong they feel they were at offering supports and benefits. The following three questions are helpful to ask:
   - *Do you feel you have had enough support and practice with the process to prepare you for this challenging moment?*
   - *Were you able to maintain your emotional control and coach the student with additional supports/benefits when needed?*
   - *Did a face-to-face conversation take place with a school leader to collect the information about the incident?*

While the school leader is gathering this information, the student waits in the solutions room. Once the leader delivers the teacher's input to the solutions room the process begins with the student developing their solution and working toward reentering the classroom. The person leading the solutions room notifies the school leader when the student is ready. The school leader listens to the student's plan and if it's acceptable (feasible, plausible, doable), returns the student to the referring educator to share their plan and asks to return to class. Closure is achieved when the educator welcomes the student back to class.

The school leader must oversee the process but does not need to spend all the time with the student. Many leaders get a bit worried when they learn they will go gather the referral information, but this saves time in the long run. This saves time because now the leader will spend a few minutes gathering the referral information. The leader is not needed again until the student has completed the solutions process. The leader will then return the student to class, so closure is achieved by the student sharing their solution with their teacher. In traditional practices, the leader may spend a good portion of their day assisting students with referrals. When school leaders and educators gain familiarity with this process, the time invested decreases.

PRO TIP

Remember we would not expect a five-point conversation to happen when there is a safety issue. There should also be a place to indicate if a student just walked out. Due to safety, the coaching is not able to take place; coaching will occur through the solutions process once safety is reestablished.

In addition, leaders may have to wait a moment so as not to interrupt the learning. Teachers will also need to understand that it may be a while before leadership arrives because they too are busy and not just waiting for office referrals. If the principal is not available temporarily, the student may need to wait in the solutions room or the office. However, schools must have a plan for whom will step into this process when the administrator is not available for longer periods of time. The student may not be okay being alone for a time, especially if they are not regulated. While a student should not wait longer than necessary as a punishment, adults also should not be expected to drop everything to work with them immediately.

FACE-TO-FACE MATTERS

The reason it is important for the school leader to gather the information face-to-face with the educator is to demonstrate to teachers that they care. It goes a long way with the educator when their leader asks them, "Are you okay?" This helps them understand that gathering this data is not so much about catching them making a mistake but rather to measure implementation of RCD and see how the school is doing as a staff. They may not always complete the five-point conversation correctly, but measuring growth is important. What quickly becomes obvious, is that the better this conversation was done, the easier it will be to get the student's brain to make the decision to be accountable.

Key Takeaways

- Unintentionally, school systems have promoted the idea that time alone will improve outcomes.
- The key is in transitioning schools from in-school-suspension to in-school-solutions.

- The in-school solutions room must help the student open the heuristic process in their brain, allowing them to find their own novel way to conquer the challenge at hand.
- The room should be located away from a major traffic area, be modest but not uncomfortable, not used to complete classwork work, and be staffed by an educator trained and skilled in RCD practices.
- A consequence must address the skill deficit. The solution must rest with the student.

MEET THE RESISTANT ADMINISTRATORS

When working with a high school beginning the process of RCD implementation, I received a video call before an upcoming visit. The principal was not always on board with RCD and often asked the assistant to do most of the work of implementing the program. The assistant too was often unavailable upon visits, and although they did not seem against the process, they were not deeply involved. Then something changed. A few high school students made a poor decision that deeply disrupted the school. This incident did not damage property but required a great deal of clean up. It was not done in anger, but these young men clearly did this to cause problems.

The principal had time to join the call and informed me they would not be doing RCD for the young men. They needed consequences and they planned to suspend them for three days. I told the principal, RCD does not say that suspension cannot be used, but that you must focus on the growth. They felt that suspension was the only thing that would get their attention. I respectfully explained to them how I would do it differently, yet I understood it was their school and therefore their decision. I reminded them I would be there the following week to see how it went.

Much as I expected, I got to the school and asked how the consequence worked. The administrator was very upset. The young men went out and had a bunch of fun for the three days while they were suspended. They even sent videos to other students to show them how awesome the suspension was. When they returned from the three days suspension, they made a masterful plan to cause another disruption in another area of the school. Their plan was well thought out this time and even included having students block the view of the cameras so no one would know who it was while they wreaked havoc. The students' brains went into the fight for autonomy. They wanted to prove to the school that they would not be controlled.

The administrators finally asked what they should have done, and I shared the RCD approach. First, I told them I believed suspension was necessary in this case due to the severity of disruption for the school and for the other students. However, when they returned, they would have begun the solutions process. Second, we would identify the skill deficit. In this case, it was the inability to resist peer pressure. The conversation with the students would have been more like this:

> You are good kids. None of you would have made any of these decisions if you had been all by yourself. But because we have another semester left before you graduate, we cannot place you in a position you are not ready for or strong enough to resist. We need to trust that you are indeed strong enough to resist the temptation to give in to peer pressure. We will ask you to come up with a plan to show how you will resist temptation the next time. Until you have your plan, and you can prove to us you are truly trustworthy once again, we will have you check into the building each morning and wait in the office until the first tardy bell sounds. Your passing periods will be at the tardy bell. All your teachers have been made aware that you will arrive three minutes after the other students to class. This way you will be the only students passing in the hallways and supervision will be easier. At lunch, you will sit in an assigned seat. It will be in a place that is not embarrassing, as we want to show you respect. Leaving the lunchroom will not be allowed until three minutes after the rest of the students are in class. If you need to use the restroom, then your teacher will call down and one of the administrators will take you to the restroom and check it before and after. When the school day ends, you will leave the building immediately. If you need to stay for any reason, then please get approval first. We don't want you to make another big mistake, because if something major happens again it could affect graduation and we want you to accomplish what you have worked so hard for. If at some point you feel you have a way to resist negative peer pressure and you would like to try your plan out, you can meet with administration to share. If it appears you have really given it thought and effort, we can try it for a part of a day. If it is successful, we can hopefully get you back to normal schedule at some point.

At this point, some school leaders may be thinking, "How will I ever have time to deal with all this?" Yet reflect on the number of hours spent trying to solve this the traditional way, only to have to come back and start all over again. The misconception sometimes is that RCD is too easy on kids. Not at all. As previously stated, RCD is focused on accountability for change in behavior and not accountability for just the consequences. With strong leadership, staff will soon see the difference and will desire accountability for real change.

CONSIDER THIS...

Use the Teacher's Words

In traditional school discipline, the principal's role when a student is sent out of class is to get them calmed down, give them a pep talk, or scare them a little in hopes of getting them to go back and behave. The RCD process works when the principal can replay the five-point conversation using the teacher's words with the student. Now that the student is regulated, this shows them the support they had and the help that was provided. This is powerful to help them take ownership. Leaders will need to stop using their own words to help the student change and begin using their teachers' words to close the exits and watch the growth begin.

CHAPTER EIGHT

Leading the Change

THE SCHOOL LEADER'S ROLE IN IMPLEMENTING RCD

The leader's role is critical for the implementation of Responsibility-Centered Discipline. Therefore, I will switch to speaking to fellow leaders directly. The time spent upfront and building this system will save you a great deal of time once it is up and running with fidelity. Schools do not need more **information**; they need more **implementation**.

Progress monitoring is essential for supporting staff while they are in the skill acquisition phase.

THE THREE IMPLEMENTATION MUSTS OF RCD

1. Practice RCD as a staff
2. School leader must oversee the office referral
3. School leader ensures that the solutions process is being implemented effectively

There are three things that are a must when it comes to RCD. First, you must practice the skills as a staff. It will rest on leadership to ensure there is both a time designated for practice and that practice is done with fidelity. The second is that you must oversee the office referral process described in the previous chapter. The third is you must oversee that solutions are being done with fidelity. If any of these are missing, the Bermuda Triangle effect will begin (see Chapter 1), and your staff will likely give up and view this as another failed attempt for change.

Heather C. Hill, professor of Teacher Learning and Practice at the Harvard Graduate School of Education, in an article entitled, *Why Evidence-Backed Programs Might Fall Short in Your School (And What to Do About It)* writes,

> "School leadership is key to increasing teachers' willingness to take up new programs and practices. When principals and instructional leaders signal commitment to a program and follow up with set-asides of resources and time to learn about the program, teachers are more likely to follow their lead" (2021).

MEET COACH SMITH

Mr. Smith was a veteran teacher and coach in a school where I served as principal. He was well liked by the students but sometimes struggled to coach a behavior without using intimidation or sarcasm. We had a challenging student I will refer to as Ty. I was told he was a problem in this district since fifth grade. He was currently a junior in high school. Ty was strong willed with a bit of a temper, and he was not afraid of any threats from a teacher. Threatening Ty with a referral or a call to his parent would only activate more of an autonomy fight for him. When Ty received his first office referral with me as principal, I allowed him time to regulate in the office. He was always willing to take the consequence but would not accept accountability for the problem. He would say things like, "Do you want me to call my dad and tell him I'm suspended?" or "Do you need me to go home for a few days?" But when it came to owning the mistake, his teacher, Mr. Smith, left the emotional control exit wide open. As a result, Ty informed me, "If he gets in my face I won't back down. I would kick his a**!" Once while in the office he even told me, "Let me get this straight. I am in trouble because when he called me lazy, I called him a fat a**? I'm not lazy."

Because RCD is about accountability, I had to work with Mr. Smith on closing this exit so we could watch Ty grow. After he was regulated in the office, I went to get the referral from Mr. Smith. He was surprised to see me and when I began to get the information on Ty he stopped and spoke. "We are actually going to do all this stuff?" I said, "Yes. But I know it is new and will take a while." He admitted he did not do any of the Give 'em Five Conversation. I explained to him how Ty was taking an exit from growth on the emotional control exit and therefore was not really being held accountable. This happened a few more times before I moved to providing more support for Coach Smith. I acknowledged that I knew this kid was a challenge and that I could see his high stress level when I got to the door. I told him I wanted to help support him and would like him to come meet with me during his next team time and we could think of ways to make sure that exit was closed, and Ty was being held accountable. Mr. Smith looked at me and said, "So I have to practice because he is a jerk?" I said, "No, we are going to practice so his behavior causes you no more stress, and so he has to adhere to his own solutions." I told him in our practice time I wanted him to play the part of Ty and let me try to coach him. We would work together on this. I also wanted to put myself in his shoes because I knew it was hard.

We had several practices and Mr. Smith was a quick learner and was getting more confident. He had another referral with Ty, and he admitted he struggled through it, but he tried the conversation and got some of it in at least. I thanked him and reminded him that this is going to be a gradual change. About four weeks later I got the message that Ty was on his way to the office. I got him settled and safe then went to gather the information from Mr. Smith. This time something was different. Mr. Smith was waiting for me with a smile on his face. I said, "Well how did it go with Ty?" He replied, "I did really good." He walked me through his masterful job of the Give "em Five Conversation and some of the progressions. Mr. Smith said, "He called me a MF and I still tried to help him." I gave him a fist bump and asked how his stress was. He said, "I feel fine." I reminded him that you can have a mastery moment even if they struggle. I told him, "You did great. Now watch how Ty won't be able to find any exit to take and begin to work on his problems."

When I got to the office, I could share with Ty all the help the coach was offering. This time when asked if Mr. Smith was respectful, he lowered his head and said, "Yes." I repeated Mr. Smith's efforts to keep him in class. "Did Mr. Smith say, 'Ty, you're upset, and I want you to stay in class with us, why don't you just go to my office or the locker room and take a break?'" Ty said, "Yes, he did say that." As Ty looked at the floor, I saw tears begin to drip to the floor. He looked at me and said, "I am starting to get embarrassed that I can't manage my temper." WOW! Finally, we were able to work on the real problem now. I explained to him that many of us have had to figure that one out, and that we will help him with this. This student only had two more referrals in high school and owned them right away when he did. This student's mom called a few months later and shared that Ty was willing to go to counseling which she had been trying to get him to do for years. Mom also shared that he told her things at school are helping him realize he should get help.

Mr. Smith was never really against RCD. He just didn't understand it or see the benefit and needed some help getting his skills in place. Mr. Smith retired the next year. He came into my office in fourth quarter and asked if I had some time to talk. He shared with me that today he had to ask a student to leave class. He did his best coaching and couldn't get closure with the student. He then told me that when the kid left, another student asked, "Mr. Smith, how are you so respectful when kids act like that?" With a huge smile he said, "I have come a long way. Thanks."

Ty found Coach Smith before graduation and gave him an invite to his home for the party. With a hand shake and smile he said, "Thanks for not giving up on me."

IN CLOSING

Teachers and students are struggling right now. We all can agree educational reforms are needed. If we wait for teacher training from the universities to change, or legislation to be passed to fix our schools, we will be waiting forever. Our students and teachers need you to lead the charge for change.

I once had a superintendent who was one of my mentors. He would let all the principals have their time to vent and complain in our meetings. Then he would look at us and say "LEAD." It is your job to lead them to the understanding that you have gained. Spending time in every type of school across this country, I am bothered by our leaders expecting things to happen and implementation to occur because they had training. Training is the start to get information to the staff. But implementation is a result of strong school leadership. If teachers say, "I don't know what you want me to do with that behavior," *lead* by reminding them of the five-point conversation and practice it in the next team meeting. Listen to your staff. Hear when they are using some of the same exits that the students use (and they do) and *lead* them to the destination of high skills in challenging moments.

Some teachers may not see the benefits until they have their own "Mr. Smith moment," and that's ok. The first change you will likely see is some slight improvement in behavior because processes are in place. The second likely change is watching teachers' self-efficacy increase as they see how their actions start to transform the culture in their classroom. The evidence of the last improvement comes when the students' behavior skills improve because of the modeling from their educators. So once again, in the words of my friend, former superintendent, and mentor ... *lead*! The result of your courage, tenacity, and commitment is a school full of students leading their destiny.

Appendix

Activity: Creating Foundations With Staff

1. Place staff in teams of approximately 6–8, provide them with a large piece of paper to record their ideas.
2. Teams start by brainstorming to generate a list of the current behaviors that are keeping students from doing their best or interfering with learning. This list will not be hard for staff to come up with. These will be all the behaviors they would like to see disappear.
3. Once the teams feel they have listed all the behaviors that are negatively affecting learning, post or spread them out on tables around the room.
4. Staff will do a quick walk around the room to see each of the other teams' thoughts. Have one team member remain with their list to share and allow the rest of the team members to circulate from table to table to hear what the others placed on their paper. (Allow about 3–5 minutes at each team's list to process.)
5. When they have completed this process, they will return to their original table and add anything others had that they may have missed.

After an agreement has been reached on the school's behavior challenges it is time to break these into skill deficits students possess.

1. Ask the teams to think of the skills needed to eliminate the list that was just created. If students had this skill . . . then this problem would be able to be crossed off the list. Example: If students had the skill of perseverance, then missing assignments and not giving effort could go away from the list. Or, if a student were able to be respectful, bullying could be removed from the list. This will help them begin to see behavior as a skill. This process will take some time so allow for ample time for them to discuss and process.
2. The next step is to ask teams to break the list of behaviors into 3–5 skills.
3. Once the list of behaviors has been created, and the list of desired skills is complete, staff are ready for the next step. Under each foundation, include a few bullet points. This is where a few of the skills required to meet the foundation will be listed. Again, keep this skill-based not "rules."
4. Repeat the sharing process by having them once again share their work by rotating around the room while a different team member remains with their list to share with the other groups.

5. When done, they return to their own team. Allow time for them to add or modify what they had worked on with any insights they gained from the others.
6. Lead staff to come to a consensus on the skills and descriptors of skills to focus on within the building.

Appendix

Practice Scenarios by Level

PRACTICING FIVE-POINT CONVERSATIONS

Directions for Practicing Five-Point Converstaion With Staff (Levels 1–3)

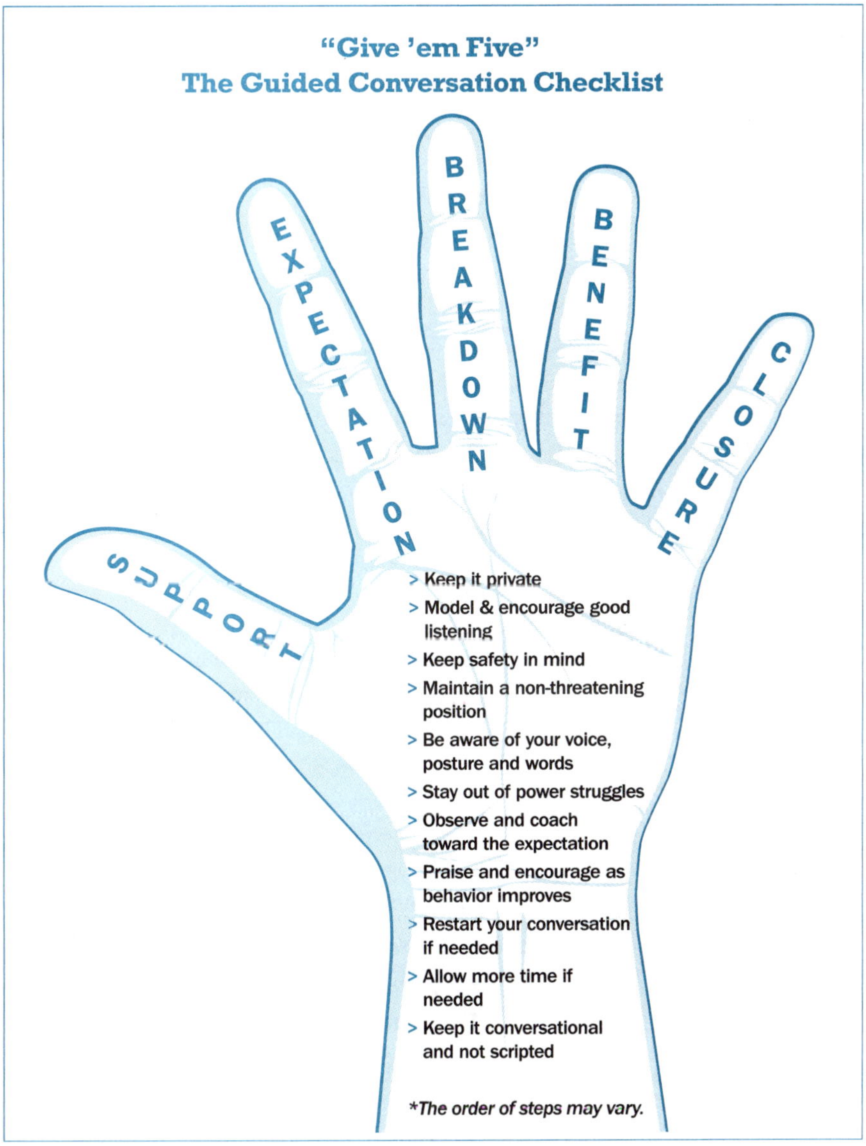

"Give 'em Five"
The Guided Conversation Checklist

EXPECTATION

BREAKDOWN

BENEFIT

CLOSURE

SUPPORT

- > Keep it private
- > Model & encourage good listening
- > Keep safety in mind
- > Maintain a non-threatening position
- > Be aware of your voice, posture and words
- > Stay out of power struggles
- > Observe and coach toward the expectation
- > Praise and encourage as behavior improves
- > Restart your conversation if needed
- > Allow more time if needed
- > Keep it conversational and not scripted

**The order of steps may vary.*

STEPS FOR ROLE-PLAYING FIVE-POINT CONVERSATIONS

1. Begin all educators with level one challenges so they can experience success. Once all staff are confident with level one challenges (see example in Chapter 5), then begin moving to level two and three. Practice must feel safe for teachers. This is where it is recommended having staff write out a scenario with their Give 'em Five, Five-point conversation. Then have them share the first one and discuss with a colleague. The second written one they would write and then do a role rehearsal of the actual scene with a partner. The third written one should be timed. This encourages participants to quickly think of how they might have the Give 'em Five conversation with a student.
2. After everyone feels comfortable writing a Give 'em Five conversation, they then begin a practice group. The ideal number of teachers in a group is seven. This allows for five coaches, (Support, Expectation, Breakdown, Benefit, Closure) each one holding a sign with their piece of the conversation, a teacher, and a student.
3. The teacher reads the scenario. Takes a moment to gather their thoughts. Once ready to begin role-play, the teacher sits next to the student and begins the Give 'em Five conversation.
4. The person playing the role of the student must stay at the level being practiced. While it may be fun to play the part of a difficult student, it is important that they remain at the specified level.
5. The coaches listen carefully for their piece of the conversation. Once they hear it, they put their sign down. So, if holding the support sign, they would listen for the teacher's support statement. Once heard, the sign is set down. This helps the teacher in case they get lost. They can glance at the signs to see which parts of the conversation they still need to include. The teacher also has the luxury in practice of calling a time out. If the teacher gets lost or cannot think of what to say, they can turn to their coaches for help. If they can't think of a benefit, the coach for benefit would help them with suggestions. It is important that only the specified coaches are coaching the teacher, so they do not become overwhelmed.
6. Once the scene has been completed and all signs are down indicating all pieces of the conversation were included, each coach would share what they heard that made them put their sign down.
7. When discussion is finished, the roles are rotated. Practice continues until all the teams have had a chance at each of the roles (coaches, teacher, and student).

When first beginning role playing with staff, provide written scenarios. Choose scenarios that are commonly occurring in your building. Providing scenarios at first saves time on-task. Eventually, allow your staff during role-play practice to bring situations they are encountering in their own classrooms to keep practice relevant for them. This will help them be prepared for the challenge when it arises in their own classroom.

Many people, after completing role play, report how surprised they were that when they played the role of student, they began to feel what they imagine the student must feel even though they are just pretending. This often opens their eyes to how certain things said and done by educators, or the tone can trigger certain responses within students. Be prepared for lots of laughter. The things kids say and do can be quite humorous.

SAMPLE CONVERSATIONS FOR LEVEL TWO AND LEVEL THREE SCENARIOS

KENDRA HIGHER INTENSITY LEVEL SCENARIO LEVEL TWO

MEET KENDRA

Possible Foundations: Respect, Friendship, Trust, Leadership

Kendra is a first grader. It was recess time, and her teacher noticed a commotion near the slide. The teacher observes that Kendra is guarding the ladder to the slide and controlling who was allowed to go up and down and who does not get to use the slide. The teacher asks Kendra to step to the side away from other students.

Teacher:	(*Asks Kendra to step to the side to speak privately*)
Kendra:	I'm the gate keeper and I can't leave my spot.
Teacher:	(*Walks over to the slide area*) Kendra, that is what I wanted to talk to you about. Could we step over here to talk privately please?
Kendra:	(*Moves with teacher*) Can you hurry? Some kids are not supposed to be on the slide if they don't know the password.
Teacher:	This shouldn't take long. Kendra, you are very creative and have a great imagination (**Support**). This game could be fun for some; however, some kids want to use the slide and are not interested in playing this game. Not

(Continued)

(Continued)

	allowing some kids to use the slide is not showing respect for everyone (**Breakdown**).
Kendra:	Well, they can just go play on the swings then.
Teacher:	Yes, some of the kids already did. I know you can be a leader and even this game shows leadership (**Additional Support**).
Kendra:	Yesterday Jacob wasn't letting some of these kids play soccer and you didn't tell him he couldn't be the boss (**Exit: Consistency**).
Teacher:	Kendra, it makes me sad to hear that. I wasn't aware that was happening. I will be sure to speak to him later about that. Thank you for letting me know that was happening. We certainly want everyone to have fun and play wherever they like (**Additional Support and Benefit**). What would be awesome is if you could use your leadership skills to create games where everyone is allowed to participate, and no one feels left out. That way your friends are more likely to want to play with you (**Additional Benefit**). Everyone should be allowed to go down the slide and to have fun at recess (**Expectation**).
Kendra:	I'll try a new game at afternoon recess.
Teacher:	Great! Let me know your idea before you begin the game (**Closure**).
Kendra:	OK! (Runs off to play.)

PRO TIP

The teacher only needed to use two additional supports and benefits. The teacher also chose to utilize the fact that Kendra is demonstrating leadership abilities as the benefit. This also ignites mastery within Kendra's brain.

In this scenario, the teacher used supports and benefits to close the exit. The following example is the same scenario. However, this time, the student will continue to exit even after supports and benefits are offered. This will require the teacher to move to the next progression: Supportive Time Statements.

KENDRA HIGHER INTENSITY LEVEL SCENARIO LEVEL THREE

MEET KENDRA (AGAIN)

Teacher:	(*Asks Kendra to step to the side to speak privately*)
Kendra:	I'm the gate keeper and I can't leave my spot.
Teacher:	(*Walks over to the slide area*) Kendra, that is what I wanted to talk to you about. Could we step over here to talk privately please?
Kendra:	(*Moves with teacher*) Can you hurry? Some kids are not supposed to be on the slide if they don't know the password.
Teacher:	This shouldn't take long. Kendra, you are very creative and have a great imagination (**Support**). This game could be fun for some; however, some kids want to use the slide and are not interested in playing this game. Not allowing some kids to use the slide is not showing respect for everyone (**Breakdown**).
Kendra:	Well, they can just go play on the swings then.
Teacher:	Yes, some of the kids already did. I know you can be a leader and even this game shows leadership (**Additional Support**).
Kendra:	Yesterday Jacob wasn't letting some of these kids play soccer and you didn't tell him he couldn't be the boss (**Exit: Consistency**)
Teacher:	Kendra, it makes me sad to hear that. I wasn't aware that was happening. I will be sure to speak to him later about that. Thank you for letting me know that was happening. We certainly want everyone to have fun and play wherever they like (**Additional Support and Benefit**). What would be awesome is if you could use your leadership skills to create games where everyone is allowed to participate, and no one feels left out. That way your friends are more likely to want to play with you (**Additional Benefit**).
Kendra:	(*Shouting*) FINE! But I am NOT letting Sarah go down the slide no matter what you say. She is mean to me! (*Kendra begins crying loudly*)

(Continued)

PRO TIP

So often in the conversation when the teacher is highly supportive the student will eventually share what the real issue is. In this case, Kendra was likely excluding others because she had seen someone else doing the same and because of her hurt feelings about not being invited to the birthday party. Allowing Kendra to take some time in the Response-Ability space helped her sort through some of her hurt feelings.

(Continued)

Teacher:	Kendra, I can see you have some big feelings about this. You look so sad (**Additional Support**). Our Response-Ability space is open if you'd like to wait there a minute. I'll go check on the other kids while they are playing. Then I can come see how you are doing (**Supportive Time Statement**).
Kendra:	(*walks slowly over to the Response-Ability space on the playground*).
Teacher:	(*After a couple of minutes when Kendra is no longer crying, walks over to speak to Kendra*) Kendra, I'm glad you took a moment to yourself. I could see how sad you were. Is everything ok? (**Additional Support**).
Kendra:	(*With tears welling up in her eyes*) Yes, I am just sad because Sarah did not invite me to her birthday party.
Teacher:	Oh sweetheart. I am so sorry. I know that can be hurtful when you feel left out. Sometimes we can only invite a few and it means we do have to leave some of our friends out. That can be hard when you are the one left out though (**Support**). Even though I know you are sad about that, everyone, including Sarah, should be allowed to go down the slide and to have fun at recess (**Expectation**). If you let everyone, including Sarah, play, they will want to play with you even more than they already do (**Additional Support**). Now, go play and make sure everyone gets a turn! (**Closure**).
Kendra:	OK! (*Gives the teacher a hug then runs off to play.*)

JESSICA HIGHER INTENSITY LEVEL TWO

MEET JESSICA

Possible Foundations: Giving Best Effort, Responsibility

Jessica is a senior in high school. During calculus class, she is seated in the back of the room. The teacher finishes setting up the lesson and has provided the students with 15 minutes of class time to work on the assignment. The teacher circulates around the room checking on student progress and notices Jessica has not started working yet. The teacher stops by and asks if she needs any help. She says, "No." so the teacher encourages her to begin her work. After a few more minutes, the teacher notices she still has not started on her work and is just looking out the window.

Teacher:	Jessica, I noticed you have not started working on your problems (**Breakdown**).
Jessica:	Could I just do it tonight for homework?
Teacher:	Using this time to work is what I have asked everyone to do (**Expectation**).
Jessica:	You know I'll do it for homework. Besides, even if I don't, I still have the same grade (**Benefit Exit**).
Teacher:	Working on the assignment in class allows me to see if everyone is ready for our upcoming test on Thursday. I can double check everyone's work before they leave class today to check for understanding (**Benefit**).
Jessica:	I understand it already! Geez!
Teacher:	Jessica, I do know you probably can do the work (**Support**). I think right now what is hard for you is persevering. It can be hard to get yourself to do something when you don't want to do it. Doing the assignment will only help you be that much more prepared for the test this week (**Additional Benefit**).
Jessica:	But I told you! I already know how to do it! I can just do it later. Get off my back already!
Teacher:	Jessica, I am going to go help a few other students who are needing my help. I'll check back in with you in a moment to see how you are doing. Let's be reasonable and fair. When I come back let's see if we can figure out how you can get this done today. I know you can do it (**Supportive Time Statement**).
	A few minutes later. . .Jessica is still sitting at her seat, looking at her phone and has not started the assignment.
Teacher:	Jessica have you. . .
	Jessica (*Interrupting teacher*) Just stay the F*@$ away from me! I'm not talking to you anymore! I told you I'd do it for homework tonight!

(Continued)

PRO TIP

At this point, Jessica would have one of two choices. Respectfully speak to and work with the teacher. If she is not capable of doing so, the teacher would simply offer the supportive 3.0 statement such as, "Jessica, I had high hopes we would be able to work through this together. I'm disappointed that was not the case. I will have to ask you to head on down to the office. I will let them know you are on your way."

(Continued)

Teacher:	Jessica, I want to be respectful of you. Using that kind of language is not only disrespectful but not helpful to the conversation. You have made it clear that. . .
Jessica:	What the F*@$! Why won't you just leave me the F*@$ alone!
Teacher:	Jessica, I can see you are clearly upset. I'd like to be able to work through this together. I would ask that we both speak respectfully to one another. And that would mean using appropriate language (**Expectation**). If that isn't possible, I would have to ask you to work with someone in the office who can further support you. I am needing to get back to the class. Could we please try to work through this respectfully? (**One last Supportive attempt**)

Appendix C

Response-Ability Mats

The Response-Ability mats are a set of three mats: red, yellow, and blue. The red mat has an angry emoji face, the yellow has a thinking emoji, and the blue has an emoji giving two thumbs up and smiling. These visuals and colors help even the youngest of students begin to understand the process of self-regulation. Young students (pre-K through second grade) who need time because they are experiencing big emotions, may begin on the red mat. Often when a child is in this space, the only thing their brain can process is the big emotion. After a few minutes, (the time will vary from child to child and with the situation) the child's brain can begin to think of something other than their feelings and emotions. Once the child is ready, they move themselves to the yellow mat. With coaching, the child is encouraged to use the yellow mat to think about the problem that had them so upset. They are encouraged to begin thinking of a solution to their problem in this space. Once they have ideas for ways to solve their problem, they move to the blue mat. When a child is sitting on the blue mat, this indicates to the teacher that they are ready to talk once again. Now it is important to understand a few things. This is NOT time-out. Remember, we do not want to rely on time to solve the problem. The child controls the time. They move as they are ready. This must be taught and modeled beforehand just as teachers must teach any procedure in their classrooms. This also must be introduced to students as a "tool" to help them solve problems. They must see this as something that is helpful to them. Not only is this valuable in teaching self-regulation but also provides an opportunity for the child to experience another mastery moment by being involved in solving their own problem. For very young children who may not yet have the skill of coming up with a solution beyond, "I'll be good. I won't do it anymore." The educator may have to offer choices by saying, "Would you like to hear some ideas that have worked for other students in similar situations?" The teacher may offer a few choices, but it is important that you leave it open ended by adding, "Or do you have any other ideas that will help your brain remember?" This allows for autonomy. Often a child may use one of the ideas but tweak it to make it their own.

Primary educators must think of their supportive time statements for using the mats. A teacher may suggest, "I am going to go get the class started, you are welcome to use our Response-Ability mats to help you if you'd like. I can meet you at the blue mat when we both are ready." Encourage young students to utilize this tool but do not force them to go. Most young children are more than willing to use the mats if they perceive them as something that is helpful. Often a teacher's support statement when they meet the child on the blue mat is, "You should feel so proud of yourself for using this tool to help you solve your problem. Tell me what you are thinking may be helpful for you?" As children get older, the mats may at some point become embarrassing for them. This is not the intention. So, for older kids we suggest transitioning to a variation of this concept. Once they have learned the process in their primary grades, this will make it easier to transition. We have seen third grade educators use colored cups (can often be found in dollar stores) that the students can stack to indicate where they are in the process. Or even laminated, colored dots, with magnets on the back. The student places the magnet to indicate where they are in the process. As students get older (fourth to fifth grades) it can be empowering to transition to the actual words you would want them to use:

I need a moment.

I am thinking of my solution.

I am ready to share my solution.

When this process breaks down, it is addressed with a Give 'em Five Conversation. It is important to remember that if the mats are used, closure needs to happen on the blue mat, even if a child ends up needing to leave the room while on the mats. If young students have experience with the Response-Ability Process, then by the time they are in upper elementary they likely will no longer need anything but can move through the process on their own because it has likely become internalized.

Source: To order a set of Response-Ability mats: https://www.givemfive.com/resources/

Appendix

Sample Referral Form

Responsibility-Centered Discipline™ Referral Form

Student Name: ____________________ Date: ____________

Time of Referral: ________ Time of Return :________ Total Time out of Instruction: ________

Initial Incident: ____________________

____

____

Referring Educator: ____________________

TEACHER

Yes/No

❑ ❑ Do you feel you have had enough support and practice with the Give 'em Five™ process to prepare you for this challenging moment?

❑ ❑ Were you able to maintain your emotional control and coach the student using Give 'em Five™ with additional support/benefit when needed?

❑ ❑ Did a face-to-face conversation take place with an administrator to collect the information about the incident?

ADMINISTRATOR

❑ N/A safety issue ❑ N/A student walks out

Give 'em Five Conversation:

Support: ____________________

____

Expectation: ____________________

____

Breakdown: ____________________

____

Benefit: ____________________

____

Closure: (Upon return if student left the classroom) ____________________

____

Yes/No

❑ ❑ Additional supports/benefits ____________________

❑ ❑ Provided time to the student ____________________

❑ ❑ 2.9 ____________________

❑ ❑ 3.0 ____________________

Give 'em Five™ Skill Development:

Select on the following:

❑ **ABSENT** *(The Give 'em Five process was not used.)*

❑ **DEVELOPING** *(Some parts of the Give 'em Five process were used.)*

❑ **PROFICIENT** *(The Give 'em Five process was used.)*

❑ **MASTERY** *(The Give 'em Five process and additional progressions were used.)*

Yes/No

❑ ❑ Was the solutions process done with fidelity?

❑ ❑ Did the student have a plan for changing the behavior?

❑ ❑ Did the student return to the class and was closure with the teacher observed?

STUDENT

(Asked and checked by administrator.)

Yes/No

❑ ❑ Did your teacher talk with you and try to help resolve the situation in class?

❑ ❑ Did someone support you in working through the situation and creating a plan to improve the behavior before you returned to class?

How confident do you feel in your plan being successful when you return to class?

UNSURE	**SOMEWHAT CONFIDENT**	**CONFIDENT**
❑	❑	❑

Student Plan:

1. How to change behavior: ____________________

____

____

2. How to allow the teacher to help them: ____________________

____

____

Yes/No

❑ ❑ Before the student returned to class, did the student meet with you and an administrator to share their plan for changing the behavior?

Appendix E

Office Referral Steps

These are the steps for the office referral process from beginning to end. This will provide the overall big picture. Following the steps, greater details are provided.

Step One: Referring educator communicates that a referral has been earned.

Step Two: School leader gets student situated in a safe space (office or solutions room).

Step Three: School leader records basic information on referral form (student and teacher names, time, date).

Step Four: School leader goes directly to speak to the person who referred the student to record educator's responses regarding implementation.

Step Five: School leader gathers basic information regarding the incident and the Give 'em Five Conversation from referring educator.

Step Six: School leader records referring educator's additional progressions used (support/benefit, time, 2.9 and 3.0 statements).

Step Seven: School Leader asks referring educator questions regarding skill acquisition (indicates: Absent, Developing, Proficient, or Mastery).

Step Eight: Student develops a plan for their solution and prepares for their return to class while in office/solutions room.

Step Nine: The solutions room staff member notifies the school leader that the student is ready to return to class.

Step Ten: School leader listens to student's plan and if ready, returns student to referring educator to share their plan and ask to return to class.

Step Eleven: Closure is achieved by the educator who issued the referral and by welcoming the student back to class.

References

Ablon, S. J. (2019). The myth of consistency. *Psychology Today*. https://www.psychologytoday.com/us/blog/changeable/201909/the-myth-consistency

Baumeister, R. F. (2015). Self-control: The secret to life's successes. *Scientific American*. https://doi.org/10.1038/scientificamerican0415-60

Brehm, J. W. (1966). *A theory of psychological reactance*. Academic Press.

Carmody, D. P., & Lewis, M. (2006). Brain activation when hearing one's own and others' names. *Brain Research*, *1116*(1), 153–158.

Cattaneo, L., & Rizzolatti, G. (2009). The mirror neuron system. *Archives of Neurology*, *66*(5), 557–560. https://doi.org/10.1001/archneurol.2009.41

Cook, C. R., Fiat, A., Larson, M., Daikos, C., Slemrod, T., Holland, E. A., Thayer, A. J., & Renshaw, T. (2018). Positive greetings at the door: Evaluation of a low-cost, high-yield proactive classroom management strategy. *Journal of Positive Behavior Interventions*, *20*(3), 149–159.

Duckworth, A. L., & Seligman, M. E. (2005). Self-discipline outdoes IQ in predicting academic performance of adolescents. *Psychological Science*, *16*(12), 939–944.

Dweck, C. (2016). *Mindset: The new psychology of success*. Ballantine Books.

Forbes, H. T. (2012). *Help for Billy: A beyond consequences approach to helping children in the classroom* (1st ed.). Beyond Consequences Institute, LLC.

Hattie, J. (2008). *Visible learning*. Routledge.

Hill, H. C. (2021). Why evidence-backed programs might fall short in your school (and what to do about it). *Education Week*. https://www.edweek.org/leadership/opinion-why-evidence-backed-programs-might-fall-short-in-your-school-and-what-to-do-about-it/2021/05

Jones, C. (2019). In-school suspensions the answer to school discipline? Not necessarily, experts say. *EdSource*. https://edsource.org/2019/in-school-suspensions-the-answer-to-school-discipline-not-necessarily-experts-say/619083

Lippman, L. H., Ryberg, R., Carney, R., & Moore, K. A. (2015). *Key "soft skills" that foster youth workforce success: Toward a consensus across fields*. Child Trends. https://cms.childtrends.org/wp-content/uploads/2015/06/2015-24WFCSoftSkills1.pdf

Mullane, P. (2022). Employers want – And will pay for – Soft skills. Are you focusing on them enough? *Forbes*. https://www.forbes.com/sites/patrickmullane/2022/10/28/employers-wantand-will-pay-forsoft-skills-are-you-focusing-on-them-enough/?sh=17e1728c732c

Olson, J. (2013). *The slight edge: Turning simple disciplines into massive success and happiness*. Greenleaf Book Group Press.

Pink, D. H. (2011). *Drive*. Canongate Books.

Siegel, D. J. (2007). *The mindful brain: Reflection and attunement in the cultivation of well-being*. W. W. Norton & Company.

Thompson, L., & Thompson, A. (2014). *Give 'em five: A five step approach to handling challenging moments with adolescents*. Youthlight, Inc.

Index

Helping educators make the greatest impact

CORWIN HAS ONE MISSION: to enhance education through intentional professional learning.

We build long-term relationships with our authors, educators, clients, and associations who partner with us to develop and continuously improve the best evidence-based practices that establish and support lifelong learning.